21st Century Yoga

Culture, Politics, and Practice

21st century yoga : culture, politics, and practice /

edited by Carol Horton and Roseanne Harvey.

p. cm.

Includes bibliographical references and index.

1. Yoga.   I. Horton, Carol A. II. Harvey,

Roseanne. III. Title: Twenty-first century yoga.

RA781.7.T84 2012   613.7'046

QBI12-600080

ISBN-10: 0615617603
EAN-13: 9780615617602

Library of Congress Control Number: 2012935841
Kleio Books, Chicago, IL

21st Century Yoga

Culture, Politics, and Practice

EDITED BY

Carol Horton
and
Roseanne Harvey

KLEIO BOOKS
2012

Table of Contents

Introduction

Yoga and North American Culture

Carol Horton

This book contributes to a new way of thinking about contemporary yoga. Nothing quite like it has ever been published before. Given that there are countless books on yoga available, this may seem like an outlandish claim. But when you consider that *21*[st] *Century Yoga* brings multiple voices to bear on the question of how best to understand and engage with yoga as it actually exists in North America today, it makes sense. Because yoga, like the larger culture it's embedded in, has changed dramatically in recent decades. Like it or not, contemporary practitioners find themselves navigating uncharted terrain. Consequently, mapping it is necessarily a new endeavor.

The roots of yoga can be traced back to ancient civilizations of the Indus Valley. As recent scholarship documents, however, what we're practicing today grows much more directly out of the newly modernized forms of practice first developed in early 20th century India. Since being transplanted to North America, modern yoga has transformed further as it has been adapted to work with the needs, sensibilities, and norms of our very different culture. In the past 15 years, this process of cultural adaptation has accelerated, with yoga shifting from culturally marginal oddity to booming $27 billion "industry."

As yoga has entered the cultural mainstream, it has been adapted to reach multiple constituencies. Consequently, yoga is now taught everywhere from high-end spas to maximum-security prisons. It's practiced to realize everything from weight loss to spiritual transcendence. Yoga is recommended by therapists and manipulated by marketing execs. Celebrities tout its health benefits while fundamentalist preachers denounce it as "demonic." Really, it's remarkable that one practice could cover so much cultural territory. Certainly, it's unprecedented in the history of yoga.

21ˢᵗ Century Yoga responds to this situation by experimenting with new ways of writing about yoga. Until recently, most books on the subject have focused either on how to do asana (yoga postures) or understand traditional yogic philosophies. In the past few years, several important works on modern yoga history have been published. There have also been some notable yoga memoirs and collections of blog-style essays. What hasn't previously been in print, however, is a collaborative work that considers the multiple dimensions of yoga as it exists on the ground in North America today, ranging from the commercial to the therapeutic to the esoteric.*

Every contributor to *21ˢᵗ Century Yoga* is a serious yoga practitioner, as well as, in many cases, a teacher or studio owner. We all love yoga. But we're also committed to thinking into it carefully, and even

---

* Several contributors to this volume have written books on complementary topics. These include my own *Yoga Ph.D.: Integrating the Life of the Mind and the Wisdom of the Body* (Chicago: Kleio Books, 2012); Matthew Remski and Scott Petrie, *Yoga 2.0: Shamanic Echoes* (Toronto: Grapha Yuddha Press, 2010); Michael Stone, *Yoga for a World Out of Balance: Teachings on Ethics and Social Action* (Boston: Shambhala, 2009), and Julian Walker, *The Embodied Sacred: Spirituality Beyond Superstition* (forthcoming).

critically. This is particularly true because we're interested not only in what yoga brings us as individuals, but also in what it might offer our societies, as well as our increasingly interconnected global community. We recognize that humanity collectively faces intertwined social, political, economic, and environmental crises. And we embrace yoga as a means of engaging with, rather than retreating from, the complexities and problems of the contemporary world.

Working with yoga in this way requires taking a hard look at it as it really exists in North America today. It means discussing yoga's vexing multi-dimensionality openly and honestly, rather than flattening it into yet another pre-packaged commodity. It demands thinking about the ways in which yoga has woven itself into the powerful currents of materialism, instrumentalism, and consumerism that dominate North American culture, and what this means for the integrity of the practice. At the same time, it invites us to honor and celebrate what we find most valuable about yoga as we experience it in this particular time and place.

21st Century Yoga is not a manifesto. Our contributors don't subscribe to a singular definition of yoga. We're not seeking to speak with one voice or develop an exclusive agenda. We hold different views on many issues relevant to the practice. And while this book is not set up as a debate, readers will see some of these differences at play in the following essays. We believe that's for the best, as intellectual diversity is valuable. Asking big questions while remaining open to a variety of answers supports creative thought and exchange by holding space for wondering, exploring, and not knowing. Providing pat answers and fixed definitions does not.

Still, we do share a certain sensibility. We agree that yoga is a practice that necessarily changes in concert with the culture of which it's a part. At the same time, we recognize yoga's potential to tap into something beyond the particularities of our time and place. We're interested in possibilities of more socially engaged forms of yoga. Yet we also recognize the irreducible importance of individual practice. We believe that yoga has incredible healing and therapeutic potential. But we don't regard it as an infallible remedy or magical cure-all. We're hopeful that yoga has something to contribute to a world in crisis. We're mindful, however, of the fact that much more than yoga is required to respond to the many challenges facing us today.

Organic Motifs

Although contributors to *21st Century Yoga* weren't asked to write on any particular themes, several emerged organically nonetheless. These include 1) *the significance of the body in yoga culture,* 2) *yoga's capacities and limitations as a healing modality,* 3) *the importance of community and reality of interdependence,* 4) *the need for ethical, social, and political engagement,* and 5) *yoga's power to change perception and expand consciousness.*

These five subjects don't represent an exhaustive list: *21st Century Yoga* covers so much ground that it would be prohibitive to list every theme. And of course, each writer has his or her own unique experience and point of view to share. Nonetheless, these themes are sufficiently central to this collection to merit a brief introduction of their own.

The Significance of the Body. It's not news that the body is central to yoga today. The average North American considers yoga to be simply another "fitness" offering, like aerobics, jogging, or weight training (albeit with a little stress reduction thrown in). Yet the significance of the body in yoga goes far beyond exercise, or even its many physical health benefits. Countless practitioners have discovered that working the body through yoga has powerful psychological, and even spiritual effects. At the same time, however, many are distressed by the rampant commodification of the "yoga body," as iconic images of bendy beauties gaze beatifically at us from an endless stream of magazine covers, product advertisements, and Facebook feeds.

While noting that such commercialized imagery exists, Julian Walker finds the positive dimensions of contemporary yoga's body-centric culture much more important. Indeed, he sees our embrace of the body as a tremendous improvement over the ascetic rejection of physicality (and the physical world itself) that was central to the ancient yoga tradition. Julian is unapologetic about preferring the sensuality of the American poet Walt Whitman, who sang the praises of the "Body Electric," to the asceticism of the revered sage Patanjali, whose *Yoga Sutras* instruct practitioners to purify themselves by "cultivating disgust for one's own body and for contact with other bodies." Whitman's joyful physicality, he insists, is emblematic of "Enlightenment 2.0": A wholly modern form of embodied spirituality that celebrates the inherent sacrality of everyday life.

Frank Jude Boccio, in contrast, believes that contemporary yoga culture suffers from an excessive and superficial celebration of the "body beautiful." Yoga, he charges, has become "a more than willing accomplice" to mainstream consumer culture and "its creation of ever more desires and false needs for product." Rather than grappling with the inherent contradictions between yoga and consumerism, however, the North American yoga community is permeated by an "almost willful denial" that it even exists. The result is a culture steeped in *Avidya:* "ignorance," or more precisely, "not-seeing." Ultimately, our fixation on the body reinforces the very *Dukkha* (suffering, discontent, unease) that yoga is designed to liberate us from by reinforcing our tendency to identify with false images of the self.

Nathan Thompson considers the nature of the body-mind connection in contemporary yoga culture in light of his experience in the yoga and convert Zen communities. Both yoga and Zen, he notes, are similarly dedicated to mind-body integration. In practice, however, both communities tend to replicate the mind-body split that dominates the larger culture. This essential division simply plays out in opposing ways: "Whereas Zen students often get lost in their heads as they strive for enlightenment, the average yoga student is fixated on the appearance and general mechanics of their bodies." Experiencing the full benefits of yoga asana and sitting meditation, however, requires remaining grounded and present in both body *and* mind. The core reason this is so difficult for us, Nathan believes, is that modern societies are fundamentally alienated from the Earth itself.

Healing Capacities and Limitations. Melanie Klein, Chelsea Roff, and Tommy Rosen share deeply personal stories that collectively illustrate how yoga can help heal some of the most devastating afflictions ravaging our society today, including negative body image, disordered eating, and drug addiction. At the same time, each emphasizes that there's no guarantee that yoga will necessarily be used in healing ways. Particularly when working with people who are struggling with or vulnerable to such problems (which, we can safely assume, includes most of the population), it's critical to be as conscious as possible about how yoga is being culturally represented, pedagogically communicated, and collectively experienced. Otherwise, its tremendous healing capacities can be inadvertently channeled in directions that render them ineffective, or even harmful.

"My body had been a battleground as long as I could remember," writes Melanie. "I have vivid girlhood memories of my worth being measured by my waist size and numbers on a scale." Unexpectedly, yoga liberated her from this ongoing war between body and mind: "The realization that I could just 'be' in my body, devoid of criticism, was a major victory." Perversely, however, as yoga grew more popular and commercialized, its cultural representation increasingly replicated the same self-alienating norms of dictatorial "prettiness" that the practice itself had liberated her from. Consequently, part of her yoga practice today necessarily involves insulating herself from the negative cultural messages purveyed by the "yoga industry" itself.

Chelsea's and Tommy's painfully intimate essays investigate yoga's potential to support recovery from life-threatening disorders and addictions. Chelsea's anorexia had taken her down to a skeletal 58 pounds before landing her in the E.R. with a stroke. Tommy hit bottom with a three-day crack smoking marathon that almost killed him. Both discovered that yoga provided the possibility for a more holistic experience of recovery than they had previously imagined possible. Yoga, writes Chelsea, "provided an opportunity to explore and heal the trauma that up until that point had not reached consciousness – despite the fact that I'd been in therapy since I was twelve." Similarly, Tommy found that yoga took him beyond the life-saving program of the 12 Steps, allowing him to "slowly undo the damage of addiction on a cellular level" and connect with his authentic self.

Neither, however, sees yoga as a silver bullet. Tommy emphasizes that in most cases, yoga will be inappropriate for recovering addicts who lack the solid foundation provided by a 12-Step program, and may even prove harmful. Similarly, Chelsea explains that even after she'd experienced tremendous healing through yoga, her practice turned self-destructive when life unexpectedly presented her with yet another round of overwhelming trauma and stress. Both agree that the foundations of recovery are ultimately rooted in human relationships, community, and love. To the extent that yoga is practiced in ways that generate and complement such connections, it will be healing. To the extent that it encourages isolation and disconnection, it will not.

Community and Interdependence. If community is that important, it's vital to question the extent to which it meaningfully exists in North American yoga today. Matthew Remski does so, and his answer is: Not so much. Unlike the Catholicism he grew up with (and later rejected), contemporary yoga "is not contained or supported by a coherent culture. It has no family infrastructure. It offers no life transition rituals. It does not marry or bury us. It does not host A.A. meetings. It runs no soup kitchens." Does this matter? In a word, yes. Without community, Matthew writes, "we'll continue to feel difficulty in connecting our mat or cushion experience with the rest of life":

> We'll be distracted by the wish to 'perfect' consciousness, rather than driving towards re-integration with the living world and each other. We'll continue to tolerate the ecstatic nihilism of New Age psycho-Ponzi schemes such as *The Secret* in our Facebook news feeds . . . And most embarrassingly, yoga will continue to market itself as a consumer-class consolation, offering a fashionable inner peace to a preciously small fraction of humanity. And in our studios, every beeswax tea-light will cast the shadows of unaddressed alienation and despair.

Such understandings of the power of community are rooted in a worldview that asserts the interdependence of all beings. "No matter how modern yoga has become, consciousness is still rooted in intimacy," writes Michael Stone. "No matter how much we believe we can be free through individual practice, that freedom is always tethered to the freedom of others":

> Yoga teaches us that as we open to our lives, we open to suffering and pain – not just our own, but the suffering of all beings. *Yes,* we heal internally; *yes*, we find more ease in our lives; *yes,* we are less stressed. But the paradox of practice is that although we feel more free internally, we also become more sensitive to the pain of others.

"Enlightenment," he continues, "is the ultimate cognitive dissonance. On the one hand, we find freedom in our own lives. On the other, we're more attuned to the inter-connectedness of life. And if others are suffering – so are we."

Social Engagement. Once we realize the value of community and the reality of interdependence, however, what do we do? There's no simple formula. But there is general agreement on the need to pause, meditate, think – and then take concrete action. "Wisdom and action can't be separated," insists Michael. "To imagine yoga as an internal and private experience is only half the picture." Matthew agrees: "I'd like to see us stop *talking* about community, and start actually *doing* community," he confesses – before launching into a litany of concrete, yet visionary suggestions on how to go about doing so.

Bc Scofield hammers home the complementary point that even when yoga works as an effective spiritual practice, it doesn't in and of itself provide meaningful ethical and political commitments. Contemporary practitioners, he notes, tend to assume that if yoga connects them to something akin to the "true self," then it will automatically infuse them with "an intelligence or wisdom that's inherently political and *against* the status quo." This, he believes, is simply wrong:

> The 'raising of consciousness,' as it's popularly phrased in today's yoga and meditation communities, doesn't raise *political* consciousness. An increase in *presence* in the world does not increase *justice* ... inner transformation doesn't necessarily lead to social transformation, despite popular conceptions to the contrary.

Cultivating an intelligent set of political and ethical commitments takes work. Making those commitments meaningful, in turn, requires action.

Changing Consciousness. If the idea that yoga's healing benefits can and should be extended from the individual to societal level is still new and untested, it is nonetheless a logical extension of our interest in working deliberately with yoga as a transformative healing modality. This is good. Yet it's also critical to remember that yoga can and should not be reduced to a purely instrumental practice, no matter how benign. Ultimately, yoga's deeper power stems from the fact that it's designed to access states of consciousness beyond the reach of the everyday mind. Yoga, in other words, has an esoteric dimension. This should not be forgotten, as it forms the heart of the yoga tradition and taps us into the mysteries of human existence.

Angela Jamison's essay provides a fascinating account of a social scientist turning her keen analytical lens first on the burgeoning L.A. yoga scene of the early 2000s, and then on her own experience as a dedicated Ashtanga practitioner who studies in India annually. "A sociologist by trade, I filtered Los Angeles yoga culture through a 'scientific' approach to practice," she reports. "But that systematic, dispassionate practice, it seems, eventually undermined my hardheaded rationalism":

> For my scholarly practice of taking the Los Angeles yoga world as just another social field, another part of me saw it as very, very special. The fact was that something *beyond* sociology was also going on there – something I couldn't figure out alone or find in just any cultural milieu. The fact was that this world transfixed me. For all its troubles, it was laced with a kind of human experience more interesting than any I'd contacted before.

Over "the next seven or eight years, or about 12,000 hours" of yoga practice (she hasn't skipped a day since April 2003), she gradually discovers that there are "layers of consciousness – many of them – that I could not even fathom for the first many years of daily practice." Angela alludes to experiences well outside the boundaries of what most Americans assume to constitute reality: "Because of repeated, usually unwanted, encounters with the weirder spirit realms, I've come to feel relatively normal about building out my awareness in the field of experience that the yoga tradition calls *Pranamaya Kosha*," she explains. "'Energy' no longer seems a metaphysical word or a purely subjective category. It simply refers to a whole world of shared, even visible kinetic process."

Reflection and Conversation

"These are new times," writes Michael Stone, "and require a new imaginative response":

We are awakening from a dream. Modern yoga is also a collective awakening and it will be interesting to see if we can transition from a personal practice into a collective voice for social change. We all suffer from the increasing paradox of living in a time whose old ways and values are dying . . . while the new one seems unable to be born. Stopping in our tracks, like we do in meditation practice, begins the slow unraveling of our momentum so we can see what is here to emerge.

Similarly, Roseanne Harvey reminds us that: "Modern yoga needs to pause for reflection. Yoga is at a precarious place where it could go a number of directions right now, and as practitioners, as a community, we have the opportunity to co-create the future of yoga."

As co-editors of *21st Century Yoga,* Roseanne and I hope that this book contributes to a growing wave of self-reflection and awareness in the contemporary North American yoga community. We believe that taking the time to think, study, write, read, and converse about where we are, what we're doing, and whether it matters is valuable both for individual practitioners and the yoga community at large. Of course, we recognize that many other forms of "off the mat" practice are important too. We feel that the time is ripe, however, for a more multi-dimensional conversation about the real and potential significance of this rapidly evolving practice. We hope you agree, and will join us as the discussion unfolds.

1

Enlightenment 2.0:
The American Yoga Experiment

Julian Walker

By purification arises disgust for one's own body and for contact with other bodies.

—*Yoga Sutras* of Patanjali, Chapter 2, Verse 40

I keep as delicate around the bowels as around the head and heart,
Copulation is no more rank to me than death is.
I believe in the flesh and the appetites,
Seeing, hearing, feeling, are miracles, and each part and tag of me is
a miracle.
Divine am I inside and out, and I make holy whatever I touch or am
touched from,
The scent of these armpits aroma finer than prayer,
This head more than churches, bibles, and all the creeds.

If I worship one thing more than another it shall be the spread of my own body.

—Walt Whitman, 1819 - 1892 (from "Song of Myself")

Not Christian or Jew or Muslim, not Hindu,
Buddhist, sufi, or zen. Not any religion
or cultural system...

I belong to the beloved, have seen the two
worlds as one and that one call to and know,
first, last, outer, inner, only that
breath breathing human being.

—Rumi, 1207 - 1273 (from "Only Breath")

Why do yoga?

Is it just about bodily mastery, or is there more?

Are we attempting to overcome our desires and attachments, or to love ourselves more completely?

Is the ultimate purpose of yoga to attain an otherworldly vision of the Divine, or to perceive its radiance in the world itself?

Can one have a spiritual experience of yoga without believing in God?

If yoga philosophy is anti-sexuality, how is this different from Catholicism?

Can we honor the roots of yoga without buying into an outdated belief system?

What is yoga all about in 21st century America?

Ariadne's Thread

In the ancient Greek myth of the Minotaur, the beautiful Ariadne gave the hero Theseus a ball of thread to unravel behind him as he entered the labyrinth. Theseus sought to slay the monstrous half-man, half-bull Minotaur at the labyrinth's center, and save the young Athenians it devoured as sacrifice each month. Once his task was complete, the thread would allow Theseus to retrace his steps – and return to the arms of Ariadne.

In the maze of our contemporary experience of yoga, I want to propose that there is a historical thread we can follow to retrace our steps as well. This will reveal a Western context for yoga that embraces the body, sexuality, emotions, reason, and the natural world.

The informal lineage of this tradition is organized around a sense of Nature as holy, sexuality as sublime, emotions as intelligent, reason as indispensable, and the body itself as sacred. Though it has considerable overlap with Tantric yoga philosophy, this specifically Western intersection with an Eastern practice has its own unique emphasis.

From this perspective participation in yoga and meditation are expressions of an evolving countercultural spirit that seeks freedom from restrictive ideology. Rather than substituting one old-world tradition for another, a truly integrated East/West synthesis incorporates the best of both worlds while discarding unnecessary baggage.

My Ariadne's thread runs from today's America back to the counterculture blossoming of the 1960s, to the New England Transcendentalists of the mid 1800s, to the Age of Enlightenment in 18th century Europe, and all the way to the dawn of Western values in ancient Greece.

Though conventional wisdom in the yoga community requires that we refer to Patanjali's *Yoga Sutras* as our authoritative source for the true meaning and purpose of yoga, I'm not convinced it's a good match.

Why not?

Well, there is a central dualism in the *Sutras* that holds spirit and flesh, consciousness and matter, God and Nature as pairs of opposites that are fundamentally distinct. Here, the stated purpose of yoga is to transcend flesh, matter and Nature, so as to awaken to one's identity as spirit, consciousness and indeed – God.

In its essence, this familiar type of religious quest values the monk, nun, *Sanyassin,* and *Sadhu* most highly as representing the spiritual ideal of renouncing a material existence that is corrupt precisely because it is sexual, emotional, and worst of all, prey to the biggest drawback of embodied being – death itself.

Sex and death dance together eternally in humanity's religious pre-occupation with transcendence – be it the Hindu's longing to leap off the wheel of rebirth or the Christian's long-awaited ascent into heaven. It is an idea common to several religions that celibacy or severely re-stricted sexuality will somehow contribute toward the possibility of not being subject to death.

Observe the holy man sadhu in India who neither combs nor cuts his dreadlocked hair and beard. Smeared in ashes from the funeral pyre to demonstrate his lack of concern for the mortal body, he smokes impres-sive amounts of hashish (believed to be a doorway to Shiva) to dissociate himself from the world around him and practices yoga wearing his only article of clothing – a simple loincloth. In one grueling ritual of self-negation our renunciate hangs heavy rocks from his penis, to damage his erectile nerves and literally annul his desire for sex.

His express goal is to break all attachment to the material world so as to move beyond the cycle of death and rebirth created by the accrual of karma. Now, clearly, not all yogis are sadhus, but we could argue that sadhus are the most committed yogis of all.

However much translators may try to soften, clean up, or water down Patanjali to fit our Western sensibilities, we cannot get around the all-important dualism at its heart. Nor should we ignore the central features of this philosophy as it pertains to why we practice yoga at all.

> *By purification arises disgust for one's own body and for contact with other bodies.*
>
> —Yoga Sutras of Patanjali, Chapter 2, Verse 40

The above is from Satchidananda's translation – and in his commentary he talks about the body as constantly excreting waste, even through its pores. It is simply impossible to keep clean, and the more we see this the more we can dis-identify with our bodies (like a shirt we will one day take off) and release our desire to touch other dirty bodies.

This controversial verse has been softened by some translators to be more about the importance of washing or of being attuned to inner clarity, but I think this is dishonest. Dualist ascetic religious beliefs vilify the dirty, decaying, sexual body, in contrast to the purity of an immaterial and immortal soul.

Though the traditional austerities prescribed by Patanjali encourage disgust for the body, most contemporary Western yogis are neither austere nor disgusted. This should not mean that we just get to change his text to mean what we would prefer. Rather, it points us toward a deeper investigation, and requires that we ask ourselves if we really identify as classical yogis.

Be Here Now

Yoga in 21st century America is hot. I mean not only that it is popular – by some estimates, 7 to 10 percent of the population take yoga classes – but that it is vibrant, alive, juicy, in a word: hot.

Well-known teachers fill rooms with upwards of 50 students at a time, mats barely a few inches apart to participate in the sweaty, inspiring ritual of shared movement, focused attention, and deep breath. Endorphins rush, neurotransmitters surge, and hormones shimmer as our bodies bend, twist, reach, hold static balance postures, and float through the air, building the requisite combination of articulated strength and pliant flexibility.

In contrast to the male-dominated old-world tradition, Western yoga classes are overwhelmingly populated by the fairer sex. In keeping with an American exercise aesthetic which celebrates the body, the fitted clothing in this milieu is often both scanty and stylish – with a price tag to match!

In the last 20 years it has also become the norm for yoga classes to feature a throbbing soundtrack of ambient, tribal, world music grooves, remixed Hindu, Sufi, Buddhist and even Native American chants, as well as poignant singer-songwriter paeans to love and loss, forgiveness, and self-empowerment. Meditation bells or deep droning chill-out tracks grace the *Savasana* resting posture at the end of class as well as the opening and closing meditations – if these are even included.

In workshop, retreat, and festival settings yoga might be blended with live music, free-form dance, and singing or chanting. Philosophically, many of the more popular "power" or "flow" classes rely either on the stripped-down emphasis of "being present" through a very challenging physical sequence, or on some very airy New Age-isms about light, love, intention, ancient prophecy, manifestation, and repurposed (if misunderstood) quantum physics.

Other approaches to the practice might include Buddhist meditation instruction or perhaps concepts from somatic, Jungian, or transpersonal psychology that emphasize using yoga as a platform for emotional healing and personal growth.

Some teachers use poetry in their classes, with Middle Eastern Sufi poet Rumi being by far the most popular source of spiritual metaphor and evocative imagery.

The whole Zeitgeist is decidedly eclectic and contemporary.

The big-business marketing aesthetic of yoga goes one step further. To any uninvolved onlooker it would appear that yoga is practiced predominantly by thin, well-groomed, silky-haired women in their 20s or 30s whose model good looks are surpassed only by their Cirque du Soleil-esque skills.

This sexy yet focused gymnast/model look is combined with a glossy print catalog representation of spirituality: just choose a soft pastel or earth-tone background, then a candle, deity statue, mala beads, or other accouterment for accent, and you're ready to go. Now, package the image with key buzzwords from this list: intention, grace, power, heart, now, present, devotion, or freedom – and your retreat, workshop, or DVD ad/print article is a wrap.

The Classical Posture

What a distance this new yoga culture has come from its Indian roots. Many purists would argue that this is no longer yoga; that the materialism, consumerism, enjoyment of sense pleasures, celebration of form and image, and hedonist group participation in over-stimulating flow classes is not what the ancients had in mind.

Yoga, they would argue, is about transcending attachments, stilling the mind, withdrawing the senses from the world around us, and attaining to a deeply personal realization of God beyond the manifest realm with all of its snares and illusions.

Yoga, they would continue, should ideally be guided by an accomplished guru – or one who is in personal contact with same – who has mastered not only the physical practice, but also the deeper spiritual essence of enlightened liberation from ignorance and ego.

Further, the physical practice is best learned one-on-one, based on the individual's unique needs, and in an intimate relationship with a teacher who has deep knowledge of the ultimate purpose at hand.

And what is this ultimate purpose? Why, finally cutting ties with this world, so that at death we no longer reincarnate, but move on to union with the Divine.

Many American yogis would argue that this is a mere detail of preference, which one can take or leave, while the adamantine lucidity of the *Sutras* invites us into living a more conscious and ethical life. But make no mistake, while the central teachings of classical yoga sage Patanjali may have beneficial side-effects in our daily lives, they are designed for a higher purpose: to limit the accrual of karma that results in having to return after death in a new body so as to work out the unresolved consequences of our past actions.

Leave this out and the internal logic of the *Sutras* collapses in on itself. Many choose instead to accept it on ancient and exotic authority. They would say that we don't have the right to critique it until we've lived out decades of following its tenets and deeply developing our meditative acumen.

But my sense is that a pre-existing supernatural metaphysics is a religion by any other name, and not merely an experiential guide to spiritual awakening.

There is also the little matter of paranormal claims in Book 3 of the *Sutras.* Through meditation we are told one can attain the strength of an elephant; develop knowledge of the sun, planets, and position of the stars; and attain knowledge of our internal organs. Perhaps a little far-fetched, but fair enough. However, Patanjali also claims that we can learn how to levitate, fly through space, and develop a body made of diamonds. He cautions, however, against being distracted by these *Siddhis,* or paranormal powers.

We can forgive Patanjali these fanciful thoughts given the superstitious culture of his time. But I'm at a loss as to how modern readers can take any of these claims seriously.

Like most traditional religious thinkers, Patanjali is a dualist with regard to there being strong distinctions between God and Nature, body and spirit, that which dies and that which is claimed to be eternal.

His *Sutras* emphasize the overcoming of the mortal body and mind, as well as the natural world, so as to identify with one's true spiritual identity and come into full knowledge of God.

From Patanjali's perspective, we suffer because we fail to recognize ourselves as *the Seer* and instead identify with *the Seen.* From this classical perspective, the purpose of yoga is to become completely awakened to our transcendent identity as the Seer (or *Purusha*) by dis-identifying from our bodies, minds, desires, possessions, and indeed all of nature and the entire manifest world (or *Prakriti*). For spirit and flesh, God and Nature are eternally distinct — and ne'er the twain shall meet!

Now forgive my Western bluntness, but I don't see a whole lot of this religious activity or ideology in any of the modern yoga scene as described above. But not being a purist, I think this is a good thing.

The Dichotomy

Here's what I do see: a vibrant, inspired extended community made up of people of all ages, ethnicities, genders, sexual orientations, shapes, and sizes using yoga to feel good, be healthier, enjoy their bodies, and explore their minds in a tribal/communal space.

Alongside this is a small group of advertisers, designers, and magazine publishers promoting a fairly narrow marketing aesthetic that is about technical perfection, youthful beauty, and impressive gymnastics.

Alongside these two groups is a third — the keepers of an ancient classical philosophy that may not have much crossover with what is actually going on in the first two groups. Sure, it gets paid a lot of lip service in teacher training. But I see a pretty radical disconnect between what is taught as "yoga philosophy" and the widespread experience of yoga in America today.

So let me be frank: I didn't come to yoga looking for a new religion. I was never turned on by religion in the first place. I didn't come seeking an ethical formula for how to be a good person, or a set of outdated metaphysical claims about the universe, God, or reincarnation. Instead, I came seeking an experiential practice of self-inquiry, physical health, and emotional awareness.

To be honest, 20 years ago I also sought to attain the spiritual status mistakenly attributed to the "advanced" postures displayed by those who had a "strong practice." At 41, I'm glad to be able move through a 90-minute routine of stretching, core work, flow, and standing poses without tweaking my back or my knees.

As a younger man, I also had some idealistic fantasies about "becoming enlightened" and understanding the true spiritual nature of life, the cosmos, and everything in it. Now I find that yoga is perhaps merely a way of meditating on my own little embodied mind and everything in that — which is actually much more valuable.

The trope I hear often in yoga circles sets up a dichotomy between a) yoga that is only about physical asana vs. b) yoga that is "spiritual" or "deeper."

By this account, the more deeply spiritual yoga is, of course, rooted in Patanjali's *Sutras* and/or in some sense of guru devotion, Sanskrit terminology, and ancient metaphysics.

Enlightenment 2.0

Though I agree that there can be an overemphasis on the rigorous details of mastering ever more difficult and questionably beneficial physical postures, I want to propose a third possibility between the devil of asana-only and the deep blue sea of religious traditionalism. I will also try to sail out beyond the shallow coral reef of ubiquitous New Age ideology.

There is already a rich and fertile context for yoga as an expression of a uniquely Western embrace of the body and openness to insights and practices from other cultures. One aspect of this is traceable to the counterculture of the 1960s, which moved away from stuffy convention, sexual repression, emotional disconnection, rigid gender roles, elitist class divides, and the hollowness of empty ritual.

The flower power generation was in search of an experiential spirituality that expanded the mind and awakened the body. Music, dance, sexual liberation, political protest, huge festivals, visionary drug experiences, and practices like yoga and meditation that cultivate interior development were all embraced as an antidote to a stagnant culture of war, greed, and inauthenticity.

While we can point out the failures, weaknesses, self-indulgence, and narcissism of the 60s, we cannot deny its powerful significance on the cultural skyline. This was the first generation to engage in a wholesale rejection of their parents' values and to engage *en masse* in radical experimentation that drew on other cultures whilst in the process of re-imagining the American psyche.

Isn't it Ironic?

There are a couple key ironies I would like to point out here. The first is that it was only in a culture this liberal and open that such a radical creative shift could occur. These kids were not in a strict, traditionalist culture, where such a rebellion would be unimaginable.

Consider, for example, what might happen to a young person in today's Afghanistan who stopped being a practicing Muslim and started doing Buddhist meditation while his or her family was at prayer.

So, the irony here is that a great deal of freedom already had to be in place in order for the 60s counterculture to demand even more.

The second irony is more to the point: The American yoga experiment has its roots in the counterculture quest for personal freedom from tradition, and the right to discover one's own spirituality in one's own way. Yet we very often find ourselves idealizing the traditionalist religious underpinnings of another culture as a kind of absolute spiritual truth, thus trading one set of traditional restrictions for another, instead of truly liberating ourselves.

We do this while blissfully ignoring the fact that repression of sexuality, as well as oppression of women and lower-caste peoples, were hallmarks of the tradition we're idealizing. While there is much of contemporary value in Indian culture, and indeed all non-Western cultures, when we fail to recognize and critique this baggage in the name of ancient wisdom — or out of a misguided fear of looking like bigots — we disown the very democratic principles that allowed liberal Westerners to turn to the East in the first place.

But in proposing what I think is the true context for yoga in America, I want to go back even further than the 1960s. So come with me as I follow the thread that connects us from today's yoga community all the way back to ancient Greece.

Let's start on the East Coast.

Of Nature and The Body Electric

As lovers of literature will know, there was in the mid-19th century an informal American movement called New England Transcendentalism. Notable figures included Walt Whitman, Henry David Thoreau, and Ralph Waldo Emerson. These poet-philosophers were fascinated with Eastern texts like the *Vedas* and the *Upanishads,* while simultaneously being passionate nature mystics and political progressives. They are important not only in the story of America, but as great-grandfathers of the spiritual renaissance we find ourselves in today.

Thoreau is best known for his books *Walden* and *Civil Disobedience. Walden's* unique ideas championed an early form of environmentalism and simple existence in accord with nature. *Civil Disobedience* says that if a state is unjust, it is morally correct to enact individual and collective resistance that would break its laws.

This emphasis on an individual moral compass, rather than one based on political or religious authority, became foundational to Western values. Mohandas Ghandi, Nelson Mandela, and Martin Luther King Jr. – arguably the three greatest 20th-century figures in the global struggle for freedom and human rights – were all deeply influenced by the ideas in Thoreau's *Civil Disobedience.*

Emerson is best known for his numerous essays – especially *Nature,* in which he espouses a philosophy of introspection and communion with a divinely infused natural world. Relying on his own inquiry and perceptions, Emerson broke with the historical tradition and social worldviews of England. He famously describes a walk in the woods like this:

> Standing on the bare ground, – my head bathed by the blithe air, and uplifted into infinite spaces, – all mean egotism vanishes. I become a transparent eye-ball; I am nothing; I see all; the currents of the Universal Being circulate through me; I am part or particle of God.

Emerson proposed that it was only through studying the natural world that we could understand reality.

Whitman was a kind of Tantric yogi of his time and culture. Like his contemporaries, he was in love with nature. Whitman was an ecstatic, a sensualist. He perceived everyday life as filled with wonder and beauty, and had a rapturous appreciation of the body. His sexual frankness flew in the face of the puritanical religious mores of his time.

Upon publishing his first book of poetry and sending it to the already famous Emerson, Whitman received back a glowing letter that included this salutary line: "I greet you at the beginning of a great career."

The poet famously boosted sales of his small first self-publishing of *Leaves of Grass* by using words from Emerson's letter on the cover. Having done so without permission, this led to a famous argument between the two, in which Emerson tried to convince Whitman to leave out some of the more sexual passages in his poetry, saying that no respectable woman should ever accidentally come across these lines.

It seemed the great man privately admired the poet's spiritual passion for nature and the sensual body, but was not ready to give it his public endorsement. Whitman, of course, refused to censor his work.

His very long epic poem "Song of Myself" is a blown-open celebration of everything Whitman experiences, from lazing in the afternoon grass, to walking in the busy streets of his town, to watching as firemen extinguish a blaze, to being in the audience at the opera, to feeding and tending to the runaway slave who appears on his doorstep, to the warm embrace of friends and lovers, to getting "naked and undisguised" by the banks of the river, "mad for the air," which is "perfume enough" for him, to be in contact with his skin.

Throughout the poem, Whitman assumes a constant first person voice as he switches from subject to subject, inviting us to see through the eyes of everyman, to identify with the common humanity in every situation he describes, and not only with that, but in communion with the animals, the trees, the ocean:

You, sea . . . dash me with amorous wet, I can repay you,
Even the earth itself:
rich apple-blossomed earth, Smile, for your lover comes . . .

In the over 1,300 lines of this poem Whitman claims everything he can evoke with his descriptive powers as an intimate facet of being-ness in which we all participate. He describes sex and death and music and struggle, earth and sea and the sunrise as a symphonic affirmation of existence.

His message could be read as thoroughly Tantric, in that the Divine is equally emanating from all that is. Yet his words are so authentically infused with his own direct experience and a complete lack of pretension or cultural appropriation, that while we may recognize the Eastern resonance, the flavor is all his own.

Though they called themselves Transcendentalists, these nature mystics and lovers of life write not of transcending the material plane, but diving deeper into it and celebrating their embodied experience.

To demonstrate why Tantric Yoga philosophy, rather than Patanjali's Classical Yoga philosophy is a better fit with this tradition I'm tracing, here's an excerpt from the 1918 Indian *Vijnana Bhairava Tantra* as translated by Lorin Roche in his book, *The Radiance Sutras*:

Wherever, whenever you feel carried away,
Rejoicing in every breath,
There, there is your meditation hall.
Cherish those times of absorption —
Rocking the baby in the silence of the night
Pouring water into a crystal glass
Tending the logs in the crackling fire
Sharing a meal with a circle of friends.
Embrace these pleasures and know,
This is my true body.
Nowhere is more holy than this.
Right here is the sacred pilgrimage

And . . .

Put the attention into the luminous connections
between each of the centers throughout the body.

The base of the spine and the top of the skull,
The genitals and the heart!
The heart and the throat,
the throat and the forehead,
the forehead to the top of the head . . .

Attend to the current of relationship
electrifying, ever-pulsating, richly textured,
between each of these and every other.

Then attend simultaneously to resonance of all with all.

Enter that glowing net of light
with the focus born of awe
and even your bones will know enlightenment.

I think Whitman would approve! Here is the last verse of his famous poem (also from *Leaves of Grass*), "I Sing The Body Electric":

The skin, the sun-burnt shade, freckles, hair,
The curious sympathy one feels, when feeling with the hand the naked
meat of the body,
The circling rivers, the breath, and breathing it in and out,
The beauty of the waist, and thence of the hips, and thence downward
toward the knees,
The thin red jellies within you, or within me—the bones, and the mar-
row in the bones,
The exquisite realization of health;
O I say, these are not the parts and poems of the Body only, but of the Soul,
O I say now these are the Soul!

Along with Emerson and Thoreau, the politically progressive Whitman actively promoted the abolition of slavery and wrote about women as the equals of men. There is much speculation, too, about him being bisexual.

Enlightenment and Romance

We can trace the quintessentially Western ideas of the Transcendentalists back even further, to the 18th-century Englishman, William Blake. Along with his Romantic poet contemporaries, Blake wrote of a visionary and humanistic spirituality liberated from both religious oppression and the specter of industrialization, and rooted in a love of the natural world. Inspired by but also reacting against the Age of Reason, the Romantics sought to reclaim feeling and imagination.

Here is Blake's poem "The Voice of the Devil" in his book, *The Marriage of Heaven and Hell*:

All Bibles or sacred codes have been the causes of the following Errors:

1. *That Man has two real existing principles Viz: a Body & a Soul.*
2. *That Energy, call'd Evil, is alone from the Body, & that Reason, call'd Good, is alone from the Soul.*

3. *That God will torment Man in Eternity for following his Energies.*

But the following Contraries to these are True:

1. *Man has no Body distinct from his Soul for that call'd Body is a portion of Soul discern'd by the five Senses, the chief inlets of Soul in this age.*
2. *Energy is the only life and is from the Body and Reason is the bound or outer circumference of Energy.*
3. *Energy is Eternal Delight.*

John Keats, another of the Romantic poets, summed up the mood of the movement saying:

> *I am certain of nothing but the holiness of the heart's affections and the truth of the imagination . . .*

The Romantic Movement, which no doubt inspired the Transcendentalists, was happening against the backdrop of the French and American revolutions. These liberated Europe from monarchy and religious tyranny, and America from English colonialism. Those revolutions, in turn, birthed the definitive American ideals: separation of church and state, personal liberty and equality, the right to pursue happiness and the freedom to believe (or not believe) in whatever religion one might choose.

They also propelled an ascendant appreciation for rational inquiry, scientific method and reasoned philosophy – even going so far as to propose the Deist belief held by Ben Franklin that if there was a God, he could be understood by rational means and would be seen to be one and the same with the laws of nature.

We cannot underestimate the power of these new ideas in shaping the Western world from around 1750 onwards. The Age of Reason or Enlightenment was the first major breaking with dominant religious dogma and traditional authoritarian models of monarchical royalty and scriptural legality. It marks a watershed moment that has taken us on this extraordinary Western journey into individual freedom.

As magnificent as their spiritual and other contributions may be, this simply did not happen in the cultures of the Far and Near East. Hence the enduring old world traditionalism in these regions, with all of its beauty and oppression.

We can trace the eventual blossoming of the '60s Summer of Love, and our fascination with spiritual perspectives from another culture, back to this first step in loosening the rigid restrictions of Christian Europe and sowing the seeds of American freedom.

The massive differences between royal families, dictatorships, caste systems, and theocracies on the one hand, and countries ruled by democratic principles and constitutional freedoms on the other, define an important aspect of the struggle for individual rights we still see on the planet today. Historically, these differences turn on the Enlightenment.

This is not to say that Western power has been uniformly benevolent. To the contrary, European imperialism and colonialism wreaked havoc on several continents. We should remember, however, that these started in the 15th century, some 350 years before the Enlightenment.

In fact, we can see an explicit connection between Enlightenment values and the anti-colonialist threads of Martin Luther King's civil rights movement, Mandela's anti-apartheid struggle, Gandhi's fight with the British Empire, and the battles for women's equality and gay rights.

Liberte, Egalite, Fraternite! was the cry of the French Revolution – Liberty, Equality, Brotherhood!

Classical yoga lays claim to being a vehicle for liberation – but it is a dualist and truly transcendental liberation from the material world and body into the great beyond. It is an abdicating of worldly concerns in favor of an otherworldly revelation, or "enlightenment."

Not so the liberation or enlightenment of the period we're discussing. In fact, we could argue that the otherworldly enlightenment is perhaps a spiritual diversion that keeps established socio-economic and political power in place.

Stay with me now, because I want to take one more leap back in time, to the birthplace of Western values.

Ancient Greece

In this culture, we find the deepest roots of Western civilization. Of course, they were far from what we would today recognize as a democracy, particularly given their abhorrent acceptance of slavery. Nonetheless, the Greeks were the first to develop a senate governing a network of city-states, each with its own local government based on direct citizen participation.

In Greece, we see the first appearance of art that celebrates the human form rather than only depicting scriptural or mythic scenes. Painting and sculpture expressed a love of the human body as being itself divine; great athletes competed naked in the first versions of the Olympic games.

It is here, too, that we first see the academy, with its recognition of the value of learning and knowledge, and the idea that leaders should be well versed in philosophical inquiry. We see an intellectual class that values reason and self-knowledge above faith and obedience to authority.

This was far from perfect. There were tensions between the priests and the philosophers, to be sure. Most famously, the philosopher Socrates was sentenced to death in the 4th century BCE by the Greek equivalent of lethal injection. He drank the poisonous hemlock rather than recant his suggestion that the gods were not literally real.

In Socrates' commitment to reason and integrity in spite of priestly political and legal power, we see an early prototype for the stories of scientific martyrs Giordano Bruno, who was burned at the stake in 1600, and Galileo, who was held under house arrest and forbidden to publish until his death in 1642. Both were guilty of agreeing with Copernicus

via reason and evidence that the Sun did not go around the Earth as religious scripture claimed.

In 1656, Baruch Spinoza was severely persecuted by the Jewish religious establishment. Under their order, he was declared cursed in every
possible way and excommunicated from the company of God and the
angels. Perhaps worse, it was required that no one communicate with
him by speech or written word, nor come within a certain distance of
his person.

His crime? Daring to question belief in the God of Abraham, and
refuting the idea of an immortal soul. In the same spirit as Whitman,
Spinoza was one of the first philosophers to propose that mind (or soul)
and body were not two distinct substances, but one and the same, and
that there was most likely no God standing apart from the natural world.

This initial pre-Enlightenment vision of a philosophical and scientific perspective that diverged from ideological tyranny was possible
only on the shoulders of ancient Greek thinkers like Socrates, who held
the discovery of truth as more important than belief in received dogma.

The myths of antiquity also carried a powerful distinction that sets
them apart from their Middle and Far Eastern counterparts. This makes
them perhaps the beginnings of a truly humanistic spirituality.

Myth and Message

Many Greek myths feature noble human heroes who defy unjust gods.
This is a unique variation in world mythology, and one that prefigures
humanism – the celebration of our human faculties of reason, empathy,
ethics, and courage in the face of cosmic injustice.

It contrasts with both Judeo-Christian and Hindu-Buddhist myths.

Consider the Book of Job from the Bible's Old Testament. Here,
the reason for the suffering of righteous people is explained as being
God's will. Job ultimately learns that the appropriate response is not

to question, but to accept and bow down to God's greater power and knowledge in spite of his entire life being unfairly destroyed.

In the story, God asks Satan what he thinks of Job's righteousness and piety. Satan suggests that it is conditional upon him being blessed with prosperity and a large happy family. So, God gives Satan permission to test Job, whose family is then killed, property stolen, and body covered in boils.

As these trials beset him, Job remains faithful to God until he is absolutely pushed to the limit, at which point he curses God for such an unjust fate. At this point, God appears and chastises him fiercely while demonstrating his awesome power. The cowering Job repents and is given back his family and wealth.

Now to the Greek story of Prometheus, who defies the great god Zeus and steals fire to give to humans. Now, Prometheus is technically a Titan, a kind of immortal deity. But his defiance of the most powerful of Greek gods is important to note – particularly because he does it as a champion of humanity.

When captured, Prometheus is not only chained to a rock, but condemned to having an eagle come and feast upon his liver all day – only to have it grow back again at night in order to start the agonizing cycle anew each morning. When told that he will be set free if he just apologizes to the angry Zeus, Prometheus expresses both his steadfastness and disdain:

You can tell Zeus I care nothing for him!

Prometheus ultimately finds a way to escape, and is credited in the myth with contributing toward human civilization.

How different from the message in Job, and indeed in other Middle Eastern and Far Eastern myths.

Take, for example, the *Bhagavad Gita's* central conversation between Arjuna, a mortal who is conflicted about going to war against his cousins, and Krishna, the deity who argues that he must fulfill his social duties in the world, while remembering that his true identity is that of immortal pure Being.

Through recognizing that he is not truly the body and that the manifest world is but a temporary illusion, that he and anyone he may kill will not truly die, Arjuna should embrace his role in the inevitable play of karma.

This particular mythic and philosophical move attempts to resolve moral dilemmas by an appeal to duty, social obligation, and the recognition of one's transcendent spiritual identity.

As controversial as this may sound, I find it important to bear in mind that the Eastern underpinnings of karma and Dharma suggest ultimately that the world is as it is because it should be this way, that we have a duty to fulfill based on our station in life and this station in turn is a result of what we have done in previous lives.

The power of this reincarnation-based metaphysics makes a caste system, wars, injustice, tragedy, etc., all part of a cosmic drama that, on the one hand, is playing out as it inevitably must, while, on the other, is a temporary illusion that will ultimately reveal a deeper immaterial reality.

If you are a member of the Dalit (or Untouchable) caste, whose station in life is to be a poor servile creature considered spiritually unclean, then this is your karma. And you should fulfill your Dharma (duty) in life and not rock the boat – in the hopes of coming back as a member of a higher caste in the next life. Of course, the highest caste Brahmins are the wealthiest and are considered the most spiritually evolved. Convenient.

When senior American yogis insist on traditionalist Indian philosophy that affirms this metaphysics and posits the ultimate purpose of yoga in similar terms, they unwittingly find themselves at a cul-de-sac of cross-purposed meaning and values. The American story, after all, is one of questioning authority, overthrowing tyranny, establishing equality, thinking for one's self, and protesting injustice.

I find it perhaps worse still to try and interpret the *Gita,* Patanjali, and other Hindu scriptures as if they were actually somehow expressing the Western values that we naively take for granted and assume to be imbedded in the ultimate wisdom of these texts. They are not. And while this is no one's fault, we fail to notice this fact at our own peril.

Even more troubling and misguided is the postmodern relativist stance that claims that we should not enact some kind of Western bias - that we are inappropriately judging other cultures or other belief systems when we evaluate them based on our ideals of equality, freedom, and individual agency.

Now, of course, we should attempt to understand all values and ideas within their context. But there is nothing bigoted or prejudicial in pointing out that in cultures that have embraced post-Enlightenment Western values, life is infinitely better for individual human beings than in those where this is not the case.

The discovery of a deeper sense of personal selfhood, coming to terms with one's authentic feelings and desires, seeking happiness in this world, using reason to struggle with ethical dilemmas, and finding the sacred in ourselves, one another, and nature is a completely different emphasis. And *this* is the context in which the practice of yoga enters the stream of American experience.

In Conclusion

I write none of these words out of disrespect for any culture, belief system, or practice. It is not my intention to put down India, or assert via patriotic litany that America is uniformly "number one." Clearly, there is much of value in all cultures. And Americans have turned in increasing numbers to practices like meditation and yoga because of the tremendous amount they have to offer.

What I have sought to do is to identify what I see as a mismatch between both the cultural context and contemporary experience of yoga in America, on the one hand, and the religious worldview and dualistic Classical Yoga philosophy of India, on the other.

My sense is that as the East/West dialog deepens further, and as yoga continues to evolve and be influenced by somatic psychology, neuroscience, Buddhist practices, and many other elements, its meaning, purpose, and context will keep changing as well.

I want to point out too, that there is a rich tradition of counterculture mystic poetry that is already part of today's zeitgeist: popular poets like Rumi, Kabir, and Hafiz all represent a potent and subversive non-dualist embrace of love and sexuality, and rebellion against received religious authority.

For example, here's the 14th century Indian poet Kabir:

> *Friend, hope for the Guest while you are alive.*
> *Jump into experience while you are alive!*
> *Think... and think... while you are alive.*
> *What you call "salvation" belongs to the time*
> *before death.*
>
> *If you don't break your ropes while you're alive,*
> *do you think*
> *ghosts will do it after?*
>
> *The idea that the soul will rejoin with the ecstatic*
> *just because the body is rotten —*
> *that is all fantasy.*
> *What is found now is found then.*
> *If you find nothing now,*
> *you will simply end up with an apartment in the*
> *City of Death.*
>
> *If you make love with the divine now, in the next*
> *life you will have the face of satisfied desire.*
>
> *So plunge into the truth, find out who the Teacher is,*
> *Believe in the Great Sound!*

Kabir says this: When the Guest is being searched for,
it is the intensity of the longing for the Guest that
does all the work.
Look at me, and you will see a slave of that intensity.

To purists I say this: the *true yoga* of which you speak never existed. Yoga is a living tradition of self-inquiry and embodied experience that has always been associated with diverse ideas, beliefs, and techniques.

Patanjali's *Yoga Sutras* refer to physical posture only twice, and are explicitly a manual for concentrated meditation and self-restraint ensconced in a dualist belief system of how God is and isn't related to the natural world. The link between the relatively young phenomenon that Mark Singleton calls "transnational posture practice" and this approximately 1,500-year-old text with its Hindu metaphysics is actually a very tenuous one. It appears that they may actually have been grafted onto one another after the fact.

In light of this knowledge, modern trends that find common ground between asana practice, somatic psychology, Buddhist mindfulness, and Vipassana meditation and even ecstatic dance are more in line with the actual tradition of cross-cultural exploration than the imagined pure and ancient lineage many pretend to be protecting.

I am all for teaching Patanjali as an important historical reference point. But I find that what gives yoga depth, substance, transformational power, and juiciness today is rooted in a much more eclectic and life-affirming aesthetic.

We can embrace nature, our mortal bodies, messy emotions, and reasoning minds. We can embrace our relationships and communities, our aspirations and our wounds.

We can embrace this limited but extraordinary experience of being human and locate the sacred within its confines – even as we lift our eyes to gaze toward the infinite universe beyond.

We can include a contemporary understanding of psychology and science in a spirituality that reflects, rather than contradicts, what we are discovering about the inner and outer worlds.

We get to define what yoga means for us in the 21st century.

This is Enlightenment 2.0.

But I will give the last word to Whitman, again from "Song of Myself":

I am he that walks with the tender and growing night,
I call to the earth and sea half-held by the night.

Press close bare-bosom'd night – press close magnetic nourishing
night!
Night of south winds - night of the large few stars!
Still nodding night - mad naked summer night.

Smile O voluptuous cool-breath'd earth!
Earth of the slumbering and liquid trees!
Earth of departed sunset – earth of the mountains misty-topt!
Earth of the vitreous pour of the full moon just tinged with blue!
Earth of shine and dark mottling the tide of the river!
Earth of the limpid gray of clouds brighter and clearer for my
sake!
Far-swooping elbow'd earth – rich apple-blossom'd earth!
Smile, for your lover comes.

Prodigal, you have given me love – therefore I to you give love!
O unspeakable passionate love.

2

How Yoga Makes You Pretty: The Beauty Myth, Yoga and Me

Melanie Klein

I can't enjoy how pretty I look if I don't feel good.

— Bryan Kest

It was in the flow of a hot, sweet afternoon yoga class over a decade ago that I realized my relationship with my body had experienced a seismic shift. Gazing up at my legs, glistening with sweat in Shoulderstand, I realized that for the first time since early childhood I wasn't searching for signs of "imperfection." I wasn't scrutinizing every inch of my body in search of "flaws." I wasn't lambasting myself with the negative self-talk that too many of us have with ourselves on a daily basis — the abusive dialogue I had with myself most of my life. For the first time I could remember, I wasn't critical of myself. I wasn't looking for parts of my body to control and change.

I'd spent almost two decades trying to have the reality of my body conform to the image that had been created in my head. The women in my family, boyfriends, my peer group and, most importantly, the prolific realm of pop culture, had influenced this image of physical perfection, and its correlating value. The joy of living in my body as a child had been replaced by disappointment. A year into a regular yoga practice signaled a paradigm shift. The realization that I could just "be" in my body, devoid of criticism, was a major victory. Within a year, my yoga practice was able to unravel years of social conditioning and begin to replace it with a message of acceptance and love.

My relationship with my body healed as my yoga practiced flourished; a practice marked with compassion and kindness. Practicing yoga didn't require punishment or a push to achieve a result outside the present moment. The physical postures operated as suggestions, not destinations. Yet, I came to understand that the sacred space of a yoga practice and the rapidly expanding yoga industry weren't necessarily related. As yoga grew in popularity and was absorbed into mainstream culture, it began to reflect many of its toxic values and norms. I found the heart of yoga to be in serious contradiction to the messages perpetuated as the branding and commercialization of yoga exploded. With a critical eye on the burgeoning and oftentimes troubling yoga industrial complex, I remained true to my practice, allowing its potency to permeate and transform my being.

Pretty in Pain

A distorted body image, self-criticism, and the pursuit of "perfection" by any means necessary is a perverse inheritance passed down from the women in my family and influenced by the unrealistic and prolific images manufactured by the larger media culture. My body had been a battleground as long as I could remember. I spent most of my life waging a war on it. I have vivid girlhood memories of my worth being measured by my waist size and numbers on a scale. Time and time again, I was taught that I must "suffer to be beautiful," a mantra often offered to me as I winced in pain as my pigtails were pulled too tight.

But I am not alone — and sadly, this body hatred is nothing new. I am part of a lineage of women who declared war on themselves, from my great-great grandmother who donned the organ-crushing corset, to my great-grandmother who internalized the Victorian feminine ideal of daintiness and measured each bite meticulously; to my grandmother who cinched her waist with girdles and ate diet pills for lunch; and down to my mother who embodied the emaciated silhouette of the 1970s and aerobicized her way into the 1980s and early 1990s with her food-and-exercise diary tucked in her purse.

This is not just my legacy. This is an experience shared by countless girls and women, beginning at ever-earlier ages and affecting them well into their late adulthood. This legacy of low self-esteem and self-objectification — punctuated by disordered eating, continuous exercise, and abusive fat talk — keeps most girls and women stuck in an unhealthy cycle that holds us back and prevents us from being truly empowered. As bell hooks states, these practices are "self-hatred in action. Female self-love begins with self-acceptance."

We've been told that "pretty" is the magical elixir for everything that ails us. If we're pretty, we're bound to be happier than people who aren't pretty. If we're pretty, we'll never be lonely; we'll have more Facebook friend requests; we'll go on more dates; we'll find true love (or just get laid more often); we'll be popular. If we're pretty, we'll be successful; we'll get a better job; we'll get rewarded with countless promotions; our paychecks will be bigger. Cultural and personal rewards for being pretty are a form of cultural currency, as Naomi Wolf elucidates in the feminist classic, *The Beauty Myth*. In short, "pretty" will buy us love, power, and influence. It will solve all our problems. "Pretty" will ultimately make us feel good.

And who doesn't want to feel good?

Media Madness

While this emphasis on physical perfection is presented to us from a variety of sources, the pursuit of pretty is most often given precedence via the mainstream media. The media juggernaut that actively shapes our 21st century cultural environment sells us this promise and perpetuates this myth beginning in early childhood. Even the toys I played with as a girl have become sexified, slimmer, and more heavily made up. The princess brigade continues to spotlight beauty and the pursuit of Prince Charming. And, let's face it, you nab your prince with your spellbinding beauty. I mean, really, have you ever seen an ugly princess, especially one that lands the guy? I didn't think so. And think about poor Snow White. Beauty took such a priority that the Queen hired a hit man to take the fairest in the land out.

The continuous assault continues as we move through adolescence and adulthood. It meets our gaze at every turn through fashion, television, film, music, and advertising. These images and messages are practically inescapable, even in yoga publications these days. They peddle products that actively sculpt our desire and entice us using sleek, sculpted models and celebrities in computer-retouched photos. The advertising industry – the foundation of the mass media – is specifically designed to appeal to our emotions and shape our expectations, thereby constructing cultural values. Advertising constructs enviable identities and lifestyles in order to sell a gamut of products and services from beer, luxury cars, and designer shoes to yoga mats, DVDs, and diet pills. And there are billions of dollars in profit when we succumb. Ultimately, we're spoon-fed repetitive streams of unrealistic images in a virtual onslaught that tells girls and women, and increasingly boys and men, that the most valuable thing we can aspire to be is, well, pretty.

And the tantalizing promises of a better, *prettier*, you are absolutely *everywhere*. The idea that we can simply "turn off" or "ignore" these messages is narrow in scope and shortsighted. Unless you're living under a rock — wait, make that in a hermetically sealed bubble — you are affected in one way or another. And so are those around you.

Given this environment, I never had a chance to emerge unscathed, with my self-esteem intact. The women in my family were *consumed by their weight and their desire to measure up to mainstream standards of beauty*; lamenting weight gain with bouts of depression and self-loathing, celebrating weight loss with great fanfare and sizing other women up. An unhealthy preoccupation with my body and food was set in motion before I hit puberty and manifested in all sorts of dangerous methods to obtain thinness: diet pills, colon hydrotherapy, fasting, legal and illegal stimulants, calorie restriction, self-induced vomiting, and excessive exercise. And all along the way, the images around me assured me that the pursuit of pretty by any means necessary would be pay off. After all, baby, you're worth it.

A Feminist Education

The truth will set you free, but first it will piss you off.

—Gloria Steinem

The routes to freedom presented themselves at about the same time: feminism and then yoga. After wandering around fairly aimlessly for over a year, running away and living in Maui for a period of that time, I had landed in "Sociology 22: Sociology of Women" in the fall of 1994 at Los Angeles Valley College. I didn't know what Sociology was or what it might have to say about women, but it sparked my curiosity. "I'm a woman," I thought and, "this should be more interesting than meeting my general requirements for a major I'm not too committed to."

"It's not you. You're not an isolated case. It's systematic and it's called patriarchy," said the radical 60-something woman at the front of the room with the "War is not good for children and other living creatures" medallion swinging from her neck. She wore a turtleneck encased

in a neat blazer and put one leg up on the seat of the chair for lever-
age as she lectured with more gusto, authority, and confidence than any
woman I had ever encountered. I was utterly smitten and completely
enthralled, all the while having my mind blown during each and every
class. The world was transformed. My paradigm shifted from one that
viewed my body image issues as seemingly personal troubles to understanding them as public issues that were (and are) systemic in nature. In
short, my soon-to-be mentor, in all her fierce fabulousness, had ignited
my "sociological imagination." And it was distinctly feminist.

My sociological and feminist education included a healthy dose of
media literacy, a field of study that was just beginning to blossom at
the time. I was offered the ideological tools and skill set to deconstruct
mediated images and understand the role of the advertising industry
in the creation and manufacture of these endless streams of images and
messages that flood the cultural landscape. This allowed me examine my
tortured relationship with my body in a systematic and structured way,
lifting the clouds of shame and guilt that followed my every move.

Maybe there wasn't something wrong with my body. Maybe there
was something wrong with the messages the mainstream media culture
proliferated – contorted and unrealistic messages that were raking in
profits from my insecurity and from the body-image issues of girls and
women around me. (The mainstream media's targeting of male body
image issues didn't begin in earnest until several years later.) The realization that I wasn't the problem was a relief and ultimately liberating.
It also left me utterly pissed off.

The Teacher Will Come When the Student Is Ready

Yoga provided the practice that rooted the things feminist sociology had
taught me. It is one thing to intellectualize self-love and acceptance.
It's another to embody and practice it, especially after spending decades
learning, practicing, and perfecting self-loathing.

In much the same way I had stumbled upon feminism's door, I found yoga. In 1996, my younger sister, Natascha, suggested we enroll in a Kundalini yoga class through another local college's community extension program. I was reluctant. I had heard of yoga, of course. After all, my parents had been hippies of the counterculture and had weathered and yellowing copies of yoga publications from the late 1960s and early 1970s lying around the house when I was growing up. But nobody really talked about yoga all that much in the mid-1990s. It certainly wasn't anything near the hot topic it is these days. I told her I was game.

She signed us up and soon we began attending our first eight-week community-directed Kundalini yoga class once a week. We spent most classes giggling as we practiced the breathing exercises along with various mantras. I think our teacher was a bit exasperated by us. But we enjoyed it and despite poking fun at it, we kept going back. We became so enthusiastic, we even had our parents join us. We'd drag them out of the house every Tuesday evening to get their breath of fire on. And, as each series ended, we'd sign up for another round of classes. Without being sure what it was, something was happening inside me and I wanted more. Eventually, the weeks between semesters were too long and practicing once a week wasn't enough. I don't think the first few teachers we practiced with that year would have ever expected that from us, least of all me.

To fulfill my increasing thirst for a consistent yoga practice, Natascha and I began searching for a bonafide yoga studio, no easy task in 1996. There weren't many yoga studios to choose from at the time; the mushrooming of yoga studios like corporate coffee houses hadn't even started. We were in a virtual yoga desert. Pioneering studios such as The Center for Yoga and Golden Bridge were too far to commute to from the San Fernando Valley. Other than a few militant Bikram yoga studios, there wasn't much out in our neck of the woods. So we ended up schlepping ourselves to the closest Bikram franchise and had a profoundly negative experience. Let's admit it; it's a bit jarring to go from chanting "Sat Nam" while waving your arms and sitting on your bum to getting berated in a sauna-like yoga room. We left with our heads hung low, feeling incredibly disenchanted. It looked like a regular yoga practice wasn't meant to be.

One of my best friends, Marla, had recently ventured out of the suburban sprawl and moved over the hill to Santa Monica (one of the soon-to-be yoga meccas of the western world). One evening, while chatting on the phone, I shared my quest for the perfect yoga teacher and the serious letdown I felt after being chastised at the Bikram studio. Marla told me she had started practicing yoga, too, and would be happy to take me to her studio. "What kind of yoga?" I asked. I clearly knew not everyone was teaching Kundalini around town and wanted to decline her offer before I found myself in another bad situation. "Power yoga," she said. I'd never heard of it and it didn't sound too promising, but she assured me I'd love it. I was reluctant but desperate. I went.

She led me to a spacious dance loft in downtown Santa Monica, a space large enough for over 120 sweaty bodies to get their downward facing dog on by donation. There was no sign out front. There was no retail space filled with yoga gear or scented beeswax candles to greet me when I arrived. An old set of nondescript stairs led to a large space with worn wooden floors above the electronics store below. The room was bursting at the seams with a sea of bodies and their body heat warmed the cavernous room.

A hard-talking high-school dropout from Detroit was leading the practice in the most conscious and loving way amidst his occasional farts, burps and f-bombs. And while I missed the emphasis on mantra and the seated exercises from my foundation in Kundalini, I had no doubt this was for me. "Power yoga" – a derivative of Hatha yoga heavy on asana and breath – left me feeling physically and mentally challenged, exhausted, and fabulous. It was 1997, and

I had landed in the company of an eclectic group of yogis led by the sometimes delightfully inappropriate and absolutely authentic Bryan Kest.

I knew I had stumbled upon something utterly delicious and profoundly nurturing for me. It had taken me a lifetime to find yoga and over a year of active searching to find a teacher that fit my needs. His street-wise attitude and working-class background meshed with my own and I felt comfortable. I was finally home.

Not only did Bryan become my yoga teacher, he also became one of my first body image teachers. His teaching fused physical postures, breath, and meditation with a focus on media literacy and body-image awareness. Whether he knew it or used those exact terms didn't matter. His rough edges held pearls of wisdom for me. He asked us to consider the health of our toes and spine, things that play no part and are not given any attention in the mainstream beauty aesthetic or fitness industry. Things I had never considered before.

I started to view my grinding workouts at the gym with a newly founded and critical lens. All the guys were crammed in the stinky weight room grunting and moaning as they pumped iron. And mostly there was a disproportionate amount of time spent on their pecs and biceps. As the character Lester Burman shamelessly proclaimed in the film *American Beauty,* he, along with so many, worked out "to look good naked." And looking good by the industry standard does not necessarily equate with health. Bryan urged us to stop comparing and competing with another . . . and ourselves. He commanded us to be with the reality of that moment and detach from the artificial images in our minds. As Erich Schiffmann states, "Yoga is a way of moving into stillness in order to experience the truth of who you are." With every practice, I was able to wipe the fog from the mirror and see the truth of my being more clearly . . . and accept it. This practice was the perfect application and accompaniment to my flourishing feminist consciousness and ongoing media studies.

Jumping Off the Treadmill and Diving In

By 1999, I'd ditched my gym membership, the one I'd had since I was 12. I began to develop a consistent and committed practice with Bryan and his budding protégé, Caleb Asch. My yoga practice became a wonderful constant in a sea of change and chaos, a place of solace. It also created a unique space to get to know and love my body in a new way. It was the first time I had ever paid attention to my body's rhythms and desires without imposing my will – a will driven by unrealistic expectations informed and shaped in large part by an ever-increasing commercial culture. I became more forgiving, gentle, loving, and in tune with myself.

Healing my relationship with my body took practice, the benefits of which were recognized that moment in Shoulderstand. That moment – with its absence of shame, guilt, or disappointment – signaled how far I had come since I had stepped on the mat for the first time in 1996. I didn't return day after day with the same intentions I had for working out at the gym – to beat my body into submission. I returned because I couldn't get enough of the way yoga left me feeling.

My practice inspired me to let go of my obsessive workout mentality. Yoga made movement pleasurable, beautiful, and loving for the first time since early childhood. My practice taught me how to respect and nurture my body. I learned to accept my body and, best of all, love my body. My body moved from a vessel to control to a vessel to cherish. I moved from disdain and disappointment to gratitude and appreciation. My body was no longer a source of anguish and disappointment but the axis of experience, allowing me to walk, run, and make love.

The healthy space yoga allowed me to carve out for myself was new and welcomed territory. My blue sticky mat became one of the few places in our media-driven culture where I could escape the endless barrage of messages telling me what I should look like or who I should be. We're inescapably submerged in an environment that emphasizes a digitally enhanced, youthful, Eurocentric, and thin image of beauty. Let's face it, our beauty standard is ageist, classist, racist, and weight-biased: a one-size only, homogeneous image of beauty available to statistically very few. In my 90-minute practice, I was allowed to shut it all out and return to myself. For 90 minutes, I was given a space devoid of computer screens, advertisements, billboards, and tabloids. My yoga practice focused on self-care, a fundamental necessity in fostering a healthy body relationship.

Baby, I've Got a Feeling

Like many yogis in North America, the heavy emphasis on the physical asanas, or postures, played a huge role in my initial and superficial attraction to yoga. Relaxation and stress-reduction are not given a lot of attention in our culture. We're urged to do, we're applauded for pushing past our boundaries, and we're made to feel guilty if we loosen our grip on the reins of life.

Five years into my journey, I sought a deeper understanding of yoga. In 2001, I completed an in-depth residential study with Saul David Raye. And in 2002, I completed my yoga teacher training with Ganga White and Tracey Rich at The White Lotus Foundation. That same year, I made my first pilgrimage to Dhamma Mahāvana in North Fork, California. I emerged successfully from the first of several meditation retreats – 10-days of silent meditation in the Vipassana tradition as taught by S.N. Goenka. All these experiences allowed me to move into the seven other limbs of yoga with greater depth of understanding.

Ultimately, yoga, a derivative of the word *Yuj*, which means to bind or yoke, is a holistic system that addresses the whole person. The intention of yoga is to unify body and mind. As Georg Feuerstein points out, yoga was classified as a "spiritual endeavor" utilized to cease the fluctuations of the mind and senses as early as the second millennium BCE. This stands in stark contrast to our Greco-Roman tradition, which

values the power of the intellect over the inherent wisdom of the body —
thereby creating a duality referred to as the mind-body split.

Not only has our being been split into the mind, or intellect, and
the body, or material, but they've been ranked in a vertical hierarchy. Of
these two planes, the mind has been, and continues to be, more highly
valued than the body, a realm deemed synonymous with the "unpredict-
able" and "dangerous" realm of nature and the feminine. Not only is the
physical body devalued; the intellect has been placed in charge of controlling the body. In essence, this enforces the will of the intellect and
tramples over the body's innate ability to communicate.

How does the body communicate? Through feeling or sensation, of
course.

And, let's face it — as a society, we're awfully disconnected from feeling in general and what we're feeling specifically. This is made evident
in Peggy Orenstein's best-selling book, *Cinderella Ate My Daughter:
Dispatches from the Front Lines of the New Girlie-Girl Culture*, a hilarious
and frightening foray into the last decade's emerging princess culture.
She cites countless studies and interviews numerous experts on body image, sexuality, and gender development.

Orenstein states: "According to Deborah Tolman, a professor at
Hunter College, who studies teenage girls' desire, 'They respond to
questions about how their bodies feel — questions about sexuality or
arousal — by describing how they think they look. I have to remind them
that looking good is not a feeling.'"

According to Kest, "Everybody wants to be pretty because that's
what they've been told will make them feel good, even though there's no
proof that people who are prettier are healthier and happier. So why don't
we just cut to the chase and go straight to what makes us feel good?" As
Orenstein and Tolman detail, pretty is not a feeling. Pretty is an outward
aesthetic based on an elusive, ephemeral and manufactured beauty ideal.

Yoga is a pathway to cultivate self-love, allowing us to shift our
sense of validation inward, as opposed to the standard practice of

measuring one's worth based on external definitions. We're able to begin defining ourselves from the inside out, rather than the outside in. In fact, the cultural validation we're encouraged to seek often fans the flames of further discontent since we can never be thin enough, muscular enough, wealthy enough or pretty enough by mainstream standards. Even if we are a waify "size zero," a bulked up mass of muscles, a millionaire or a picture-perfect model, happiness isn't a guarantee. There are plenty of depressed, disgruntled, unsatisfied "pretty people" with low self-esteem.

"Pretty" doesn't necessarily signal a healthy body, mentally or physically. In fact, in my own work as a body image activist, many of the most "beautiful" women I've met have had some of the most dysfunctional and unhealthy relationships with their bodies. Too often, this has been marked by disordered eating and dangerous beauty rituals to maintain the outward facade. In the end, there isn't a direct correlation between being pretty and being happy or healthy. The prizes "pretty" entices us with can't be enjoyed without a deeper connection, a feeling of wellness, wholeness and/or self-love. Pretty hasn't delivered and what has been defined as pretty isn't real or sustainable.

Remember, Naomi Wolf called it the "beauty myth" for a reason.

Broken Mirror

Countless studies have revealed that meditation makes you feel good. The heart and life force of yoga is the breath. It is the focal point that transforms the physical movements, or asanas, into a moving meditation that distinguishes it from other forms of exercise. Ultimately, yoga is defined by quality of mind, not one's ability to move further into a Backbend or perfect Headstand. As Kest reminds us, without the focused breath, or pranayama, which ultimately cultivates that distinct state of mind, yogic postures are "just silly eastern calisthenics." By remaining committed to my breath and not approaching my time on the mat as a

competitive sport or a beauty competition, I engaged in a practice that
ran counter to everything I had been taught my whole life.

This fresh approach allowed me to become aware of and accept the
"fat days" and, most importantly, move beyond them. Years earlier, I
would have succumbed to them, thereby becoming debilitated. Often I
would cancel commitments, because I didn't want to leave my house on
those days. As body image activist, Jessica Weiner, famously proclaims
"life doesn't begin five pounds from now." Yoga helped me understand
that on a visceral level.

Yoga also helped me identify the truth in the midst of a distorted
body image. One's body image has little to do with the reality of one's
reflection in the mirror. Body image is a highly subjective psychological
image of one's self that is cobbled together from a lifetime of experiences. My practice allowed me to move beyond those crippling moments
where I felt huge and unlovable by teaching me how to be with my body
moment to moment. In that, I was able to identify my fleeting and un-
stable body image sentiments understanding that they were imperma-
nent and fallacious. This provided immense freedom.

Feminism and yoga raised my consciousness and led me back to myself in love. The distorted image in the mirror had been shattered. I
attribute these two complimentary systems for suturing the emotional
and physical wounds and saving my life.

But while I was healing from my body image battle scars, the corporate machine was bifurcating the practice of yoga from the culture
of yoga.

Yoga Goes Pop!

Inevitably, yoga was absorbed by the larger mainstream culture. Yoga
studios popped up like Starbucks coffee houses, and an endless array
of yoga apparel filled their lobbies. In many ways, yoga became more
about how you looked in your color-coordinated outfit than the practice

itself. Slowly, yoga became filtered through and reflected the dominant consciousness, a consciousness informed by corporate consumerism aimed at maximizing profit by any means necessary.

While I was skeptical and increasingly critical of this (de)evolution, I did welcome several aspects of this yoga/pop-culture marriage. I was grateful that more people became exposed to yoga, many of whom might have never given yoga a chance otherwise. I also appreciated access to yoga products that did not exist previously, or were hard to come by just a few years before.

With that said, I became dismayed by the marketing tactics used by corporate advertisers. The types of products being advertised in mainstream yoga publications changed rapidly once the momentum began, complemented by credit cards ads featuring mantra-chanting yogis. I became increasingly disillusioned and disappointed.

I began making public commentary on these changes beginning in 2003, presenting papers at a variety of sociological conferences and public lectures with titles such as:

- *Celebrity Yogis: The Intersection of Yoga, the Cult of Personality and Consumerism*
- *Yoga and Popular Culture, McYoga: The Spiritual Diet for Consumer America*
- *Consuming Spirituality and Spiritual Consuming: Capitalizing on Yoga*
- *The McDonaldization and Commodification of Yoga: Standing at the Intersection of Spiritual Tradition and Consumer Culture.*

I was particularly interested in the reproduction of mainstream beauty standards in the pages of yoga magazines. Mirroring the dominant culture, yoga's cover models feature little diversity in terms of size, age, and race. Virtually every model is young, thin, white and super-polished. In fact, this is the case not only in advertisements and publications geared to yogis, but in the art of popular yoga photography.

After examining the mainstreaming of yoga for several years with frustration and sadness, I put down the yoga magazines and withdrew from the increasingly commercialized yoga community. The community that had previously provided me with self-acceptance began to increasingly reflect the mainstream culture from which I sought solace. What sealed the deal for me is when I stumbled upon an advertisement for diet pills in *Yoga Journal.*

Not only had yoga publications succumbed to accepting corporate dollars for products that seemed unrelated to a healthy yogic lifestyle, but now they'd allowed the ultimate self-esteem crusher to enter: advertisements reinforcing larger cultural messages focused on size, not health. This trend continues with yoga ads, DVDs, and products that focus solely on weight loss, such as the recent ad promising a yogi-slim body in the form of a "size zero" and the continued use of models that don't reflect the diverse range of women and men practicing and teaching yoga.

In my opinion, the relentless focus on weight loss and the advertising of diet pills has no place in yoga. It runs counter to cultivating the unique quality of the practice that fosters healthy minds and bodies, which is what yoga is about. It changes the quality of yoga and detracts from yoga's true power to transform from within. Without that certain quality of mind, it's not yoga. Yoga becomes reduced to just another form of working out, a means to an end. Yoga is more than just a pretty face and slim body in a designer yoga outfit.

To Thine Own Self Be True

I've vowed to preserve the uncluttered space a yoga practice provides, the rare space devoid of manufactured messages telling us who we should be and promising us those illusive dreams through the sale of a product. We get enough of those outside yoga. My Tantric Dance of Feminine Power teacher, Nita Rubio, encourages her students to "let go of the pretty," or the external veneer, in order to tap into the wealth of sensation offered by the body. This is where personal power and innate bodily wisdom can be accessed. This is yoga. This is the root of transformation. I've vowed to preserve my healing sanctuary by separating my yoga practice from the yoga industry and eyeing that industry critically.

As I breathe and move through asana, I practice forgiveness, acceptance, tolerance, compassion, understanding, and self-acceptance. This has ultimately led me to self-love, a gift available to all. Self-love is a feeling that blossoms and radiates outward. It allows us to love ourselves unconditionally. And therein, true beauty is revealed.

I have vowed to preserve my practice amidst the increasing corporate noise. I've vowed to remain true to myself. This is my intention: to feel beautiful, rather than merely looking pretty.

3

Questioning the "Body Beautiful": Yoga, Commercialism, and Discernment

Frank Jude Boccio

In contemporary North American yoga, the physical postural practice of Hatha yoga has commonly become synonymous with yoga. For most practitioners, when they say they practice yoga, what they really mean is that they practice asana. Recently, *Yoga Journal* asked its readers, "Where's the most unusual place you've practiced yoga?" Both the question itself and answers given made it obvious that everyone was thinking of postures. If one adheres to the wider understanding of yoga as meditation, integrated practice, and yoked (unified) action, however, my response to the magazine's query might be changing my daughter's diaper in the vestibule of a Catholic church.

Now, perhaps one's position on the contemporary situation is that this is fine, that it's a sign of yoga's ability to evolve. Focusing on the physical practice of asana, it's frequently said, allows yoga to become more accessible to more people. The problem with this, however, is that when people begin to experience the potential negatives of a physically focused practice, such as injuries or the simple changes in body states and abilities that come with age, many of these same people will drop the practice. We see this happening already, with total participation in yoga over the past two years reportedly shrinking two million from a high of 16 million.

One who voices the opinion that to equate yoga with asana reduces the breadth and depth of the "yoga tradition," and often leads to a misuse of the practice, places himself in a critical relationship to the mainstream status quo. For taking this position, I've personally been called a "purist," which is ironic, as I've jettisoned much of the traditional metaphysics and philosophical underpinning of yoga. What I have retained is a tremendous respect for the ability of the practices of yoga to lead to profound freedom and self-awareness.

As I write this in January 2012, the current storm in the yoga blogosphere (there seems to be one at least every season) is over an article published in the *New York Times* entitled "How Yoga Can Wreck Your Body." Predictably, those who have been injured, and those who work with practitioners who have been injured, find the article a breath of fresh air, exposing the shadow side of contemporary yoga practice. Others criticize the article for its histrionic hyperbole. These "true believers" offer the litany of health benefits asana practice can deliver and point out the very real factual errors and misconceptions within the article.

From my perspective, both sides have valid points. However, in reviewing over a dozen responses to the article, I saw only one that pointed out that the article should have more accurately been titled "How Asana Can Wreck Your Body." The whole controversy seems to painstakingly avoid the more pressing issue I wish to address: that is, the body-centric orientation so prevalent in North American yoga today.

The Social Context of the Body

But first, a word about this tendency to avoid what I see as the crux of the matter. The various yoga traditions all seem to agree that the major cause of *Dukkha* (suffering, discontent, unease, etc.) is *Avidya,* a word that's often translated as "ignorance." This translation implies some specific lack of knowledge. And while that may be so, it leaves aside the idea of "ignore-ance" or "denial," concepts that come much closer to the literal translation of *Avidya* as "not-seeing." Understood in this way, *Avidya* means to willfully deny or ignore issues, questions, or even ambiguities that may have uncomfortable implications for our actions, beliefs, and practices. We see only what makes us feel most immediately comfortable, and refuse to contemplate what does not.

Avidya is pervasive in the contemporary yoga world precisely because of its overly body-centric orientation. Contemporary yoga culture is marked by a widespread refusal to "see" troubling issues generated by its insistent celebration of bodies considered "beautiful" by dominant cultural standards – thin, toned, light-skinned, conventionally pretty young women with gymnastic-like skills in particular. A recent example of this can be seen in the response to critiques of the "Yoga by Equinox" video, an online advertisement for Equinox fitness clubs that currently has almost four million views. This viral video features a young, attractive, and exceptionally athletic yoga instructor performing a highly demanding asana series clad only in stylish black lingerie. Adding to the ambiance is the fact that her mat is stretched out in front of a huge, rumpled bed in which a man lies sleeping, all comfortably ensconced in a lushly minimalist, expensive-looking urban penthouse apartment.

"Yoga by Equinox" generated a small firestorm in the online yoga community. Not surprisingly, some critiqued it as yet another example of yoga being reduced to a marketable commodity representing dominant conceptions of physical attractiveness and desirability. In the online world, however, public opinion is measured by views and click-throughs – and in those terms, "Yoga by Equinox" was nothing if not a monumental success. Nonetheless, many yoga practitioners felt moved to respond to its critics by writing impassioned defenses of the video and posting them online.

Popular American yoga teacher Kathryn Budig emerged as a leading spokeswoman countering the critics. In a widely noted *Huffington Post* article entitled "Stop Judging and Read," Budig explains that she felt compelled to defend the teacher featured in the video because she herself had suffered through an onslaught of negative "judgments" for posing in a series of advertisements wearing nothing but "yoga socks." In her view, the motivation behind these ads was simple, positive, and constructive: "Our intention was to inspire and show the beauty of a body that practices regular yoga to get people back on their mats."

Budig goes on to note, however, that "there are two sides to the coin and many people were displeased" with the advertising campaign. Criticisms, she reports, included observations that such advertisements objectify women, use sex to sell product, and are offensive. In response, she states simply that: "My intention was to inspire and empower and I knew that desired effect had taken place. I also knew if you stick your head above a crowd, someone's bound to throw a tomato at it."

I'd argue, however, that there's a reason that "intention" comes *after* "understanding" in the Buddha's Noble Eightfold Path: intention alone, without understanding, can cause much suffering. There are many excellent books and articles documenting that the 12 hours or more of media imagery seen by the average American daily has a negative effect on the psychological development of girls and women. The documentary film, *Miss Representation,* similarly shows how the media's emphasis on women's appearance and sexual desirability locates the value of a woman *in* her appearance. This message is not lost on young boys who grow up to be men who value women primarily for their bodies – that is, as long as they look like the images they've been presented with by the media. Given such toxic cultural bombardment, is it any wonder that 90 percent of all junior and senior high school girls are on a diet, while only

15 percent of these girls are actually overweight? Or that 90 percent of American women report disliking their bodies?

To "not see" the significance of such powerful cultural realities constitutes *Avidya*. This remains true regardless of our intentions. We may sincerely believe that if advertisements featuring culturally iconic images of "beautiful bodies" are associated with yoga, then they will have only a positive effect. We may truly desire to "inspire" others to practice by advertising "the beauty of a body that practices regular yoga." Such commitments beg the question, however, of whether reinforcing the already epidemic desire to conform to media-anointed standards of the "body beautiful" is truly compatible with yoga.

An Obstacle to Liberation?

That a body-centric emphasis would develop in contemporary North American yoga is not surprising. When I was first introduced to yoga in the mid-1970s, we were often told that asana was practiced as preparation for meditation, yet we never got to meditate in class. Even at the ashram where I took classes, meditation instruction and practice was offered in separate classes and no attempt to integrate asana and meditation was ever made. Not surprisingly, the meditation classes were always sparsely attended, while the asana classes were packed. Still, the asana practice then was generally not about being athletically challenging, and there was little emphasis on attaining some ideal form. Asana was mostly about feeling good, and not so much about looking good. Of course, yoga is about much more than feeling good, but at least at the ashram there was no perceived or actual pressure to feel better than the next yogi!

This was before some folks figured out there was money to be made from yoga, so there was little of the targeted advertising and marketing of product that some say has made yoga more accessible. That may be so, but at what cost? Is it possible that yoga has become so co-opted by mainstream culture that it is losing – or has already lost – its radical countercultural potential?

I believe that it has. Rather than questioning the capitalist model of consumerism, with its creation of ever more desires and false needs for product, contemporary yoga has become a more than willing accomplice. Rather than presenting an alternative to the concomitant ideology of North American individualism, which prioritizes and valorizes the isolated "self" over the relational matrix, it has eagerly embraced it.

In the *Yoga Journal* I have in front of me as I write this, I count at least 21 large ads for fashion accessories, with seven featuring scantily clad or provocatively posed white, thin women and five ads for various "beauty" products. One ad promotes its product with several slogans including "Standout in comfort," "Especially me," and "Be yourself, be naturally beautiful." Another suggests that you can "Find your inner peace. For less." It goes on to assert: "Nothing calms the mind like saving money." Really? *Nothing?* And you get to save by buying their advertised product?

While others have written extensively about the effects of advertising and the commodification of women's bodies to sell product, what I wish to address here is an un-thinking, feel-good "celebration of the body" that has also been incorporated into contemporary yoga. I believe this seemingly positive celebration of the body is merely a specific cultural and historical manifestation of the shadow side of Hatha yoga and its historical tendency to fixate on the body.

As early as the 10th century, the *Garuda-Purana,* which the *Brhadaranyaka Upanishad* refers to as the "Fifth Veda," warned that "the techniques of posture do not promote yoga. Though called essentials, they all retard one's progress." Now, that's a pretty strong, unrestrained, and perhaps even a bit damningly harsh statement. It's asserting that a fixation on the physical, rather than being a mere distraction or diversion, can be a total and complete *obstacle* to liberation! By these standards, yoga as practiced and conceived of by the contemporary mainstream is actually an impediment to liberation. Today's contemporary sell-out glorification of the body seems to prove this. In fact, many practitioners of popular yoga may have little, if any idea of *Dukkha* and the soterio-logical purpose of yoga practice to free us from it — and equal ignore-ance of the *Dukkha* their "feel-good" celebration actually perpetuates and encapsulates.

What Makes a Body "Beautiful"?

Yoga aims to break our identification with body or mind as "self." The physically oriented approach to Hatha yoga so prevalent today all too often strengthens practitioners' identification with the body — what it looks like and what one can or cannot do with it. There is a strong focus on attaining idealized, and ever more "challenging" or "advanced" postures — and the concomitant pride that comes from doing so. When ego is invested in what the body does, injuries are often the result. *That's* how asana (yoga) can wreck your body! There is also the discouragement many feel when they realize that they simply cannot do a posture. Also, of course, is the reality that whether from age, injury, or illness (not to mention death) one day you will not be able to practice the postures you may have taken pride in achieving. What happens then?

When we unthinkingly accept the pop cultural valuation of "the body beautiful" that permeates contemporary yoga, we stop looking deeper. We stop at the surface of appearance and paradoxically lose in-timacy with the body *as* body. Yoga opens the door to true intimacy by questioning our unconscious assumptions. It asks, *"Is* the body beauti-ful?" Really? Yoga asks us to look further. Without denying its beauty, can you ask, "Is the body *only* beautiful?"

Budig has stated her intention as wanting "to inspire and show the beauty of a body that practices regular yoga to get people back on their mats." It is just as likely that someone whose body is nothing like hers could feel discouragement instead. *My* body isn't like hers. It cannot do all that her body can! This very emphasis on the physical and per-formance of postures can actually make yoga inaccessible for many who could truly benefit from an integrated yoga practice. If looking good naked is the motivation to "get back on the mat," then it's truly a sad commentary on the depth of yoga practice in contemporary North America.

What yogis like the Buddha point out is that such concepts as "beauty" (as well as "the body") are conditioned and empty of any inherent nature or essence. For all those who argue that contemporary yoga is empowering by celebrating the body, and that the ads featuring nearly or completely nude women are beautiful because they portray "the beauty of the human body," it may be enlightening to ask: *Really?* Then why not portray a 64-year-old man with a bit of a belly roll? How about a nice nude shot of the character George Constanza – or Newman – from *Seinfeld?* Would you then argue for "the beauty of the human body?" As much as I would like to think people would be consistent in their approval, I cannot help but doubt it.

And why would it be highly unexpected to see such photos? While the ads and covers, few and far between, that occasionally appear in *Yoga Journal* featuring African American or Asian or full-bodied women are applauded for showing contemporary yoga's diversity and inclusivity, the very fact that their appearance sparks comment is evidence of the social conditioning we so often remain blind to and to the secondary status of the ignored.

While there has been occasional criticism of contemporary yoga's unquestioning adoption of the mainstream consumerist culture, as well as some questioning of using images of scantily clad women to sell product, what isn't talked about is the unthinking celebration of the "body beautiful." In fact, though, our ideals of beauty are culturally and biologically conditioned. Folks somewhat facilely use abstract concepts, get caught up in them, and then fail to see all that is under erasure. This is what psychoanalyst Jeffrey Rubin calls "the blindness of the seeing I."

So, for the sake of argument, let's posit that one does see beauty in all bodies, including a naked George Constanza or Newman. What I propose to do here is to analyze the position so frequently celebrated and so baldly stated as "the body is beautiful" more deeply. I am not arguing that the body is *not* beautiful. But I do suggest that we need to also remember (be mindful — the word *Sati,* which is often translated as "mindfulness" actually means "to remember") that it isn't *only* beautiful. Depending on circumstances, the body can often be perceived as much less than beautiful, even gross at times. For instance, this "body" that contemporary yoga celebrates takes quite a bit of maintenance. Just go a few weeks without bathing and tell me how beautiful you think the body is.

When we are shown a "beautiful" woman, with long lustrous locks, we may immediately think, "Wow, she has such lovely hair." And yet, what might be your reaction if you found one of her hairs in your soup? Would you find *that* hair beautiful? And as the model is naked, how would you feel if it were one of her pubic hairs? What if that lustrously long hair were sprouting from her chin? Still celebrating the "beauty of the human body?" And how delighted are you to be cleaning her hair from your shower drain?

Interdependence and Collectivity

Quite simply, the point I wish to make is that what yoga offers us is a clearer, more complete understanding of reality: *Samprajanya,* clear comprehension, and *Viveka,* discernment. The surface and general form of the body we are made to feel is beautiful because of our biological conditioning. Our survival as a species, it has been argued, depends upon this biological conditioning. Additionally, there are specific cultural norms that condition our ideas of beauty. Unfortunately, in the 21st century, most images of beauty presented by mainstream media in North America are white, thin, and female. This is cultural conditioning. And as such, it is generally ignored (not-seen) because of its being conditioned. That's the reason the slogan, "Black is beautiful," had to be created and given voice. And it's why it struck such a provocative and resonant tone when it was first articulated during the age of slavery, as well as in the 1960s.

But the great yogis point out that the body is inherently neither beautiful *nor* disgusting. As the *Heart of the Prajnaparamita Sutra* declares about reality, it is "Neither produced nor destroyed; neither pure nor impure; neither increasing nor decreasing." Get that? Not pure; not impure. Beauty arises with the coming together of many causes and conditions that create what we think of as "beauty." That woman's lustrous, "beautiful" hair is not inherently beautiful; it's beautiful because the conditions (among them being: it's on her head, it's clean, the rest of her face is harmonious, and we've been culturally conditioned to see long, wavy hair positively) are all present. The "beauty" is a construct, interdependently created. And with the coming together of other, different causes and conditions, the perception of what we think of as "ugliness" is created.

The next time you catch yourself thinking someone has beautiful eyes, contemplate briefly if the beauty is really inherent in their eyes. Would you think they were beautiful if s/he plucked them out and handed them to you? Or is beauty created (conditioned or constructed) because the eyes are in their "proper" place: they are balanced and relatively symmetrical, and the rest of her or his face is pleasing. *All* phenomena arise interdependently. This is what is meant by "form being empty." We need to ask, "empty of what?" And the answer is: "empty of an inherent self-essence." This insight is necessary if we are ever to become free of the grasping and clinging, as well as the aversion, that causes so much suffering.

We can perform a similar investigation into the very concept of "the body." While it seems unitary, independent, autonomous, and persistent, just a little mindfulness meditation on the body (what the Buddha called "the First Foundation of Mindfulness") will reveal that it is more accurate to think of the body as a form of collective. It is made of many parts, organs, systems, tissues, and cells. If we extract the DNA from one's body, we find that 90 percent is non-human. There are so many non-human organisms living on and in the body that their DNA makes up 90 percent of our body. Yet, without them, we could not live! So, what really defines "your" body?

The body is not unitary. It isn't independent (try not eating for a couple of months) and certainly not autonomous. If it were, as the Buddha pointed out, you could say "Let it be thus, and it would be thus." Yeah, if only! And all it takes is a moment to look at your baby photos – or even the photos of what you looked like ten years ago – to see it doesn't persist unchangingly. The body is not "self," yet when we fixate on the body, that is just what we take it to be.

Freedom and Intimacy

If we merely stop and proclaim the beauty of the human body, we fail to go deeper. We fail to see reality and instead get caught in grasping and clinging. Freedom – the purpose of yoga practice, after all – is to go beyond such conditioning. This does not mean that we stop appreciating the human form. What is changed is the quality of our relationship to the body, and to all beings. Going beyond the surface, we reach a much deeper intimacy. Dogen, the great 14th century Zen master wrote, "*Zazen* (sitting meditation) is the investigation of the self. Investigating the self, we forget the self. In forgetting the self, we become intimate with all things."

My wife told me of a dream she had years ago, at the beginning of our relationship, before we had made our commitment to each other. She dreamt her guts were spilling out, and she was experiencing mortifying shame and embarrassment that they were being exposed to my gaze. And, within her dream, she experienced an upwelling of love and gratitude as, with no sign of revulsion, I helped her to put her guts back in place.

I share this only to offer a vivid image offered up by the unconscious of the kind of unconditional love yoga offers us. When my wife shared this dream image with me, I knew her intuitive mind had revealed a truth about my love for her. But in order to open to this kind of love, we need "to see things as it is," as Suzuki Roshi would often say. And advertising and unquestioned assumptions about things – including the body – NEVER show us things as they are!

4

Bifurcated Spritualties: Mind/Body Splits in the North American Yoga and Zen Communities

Nathan G. Thompson

During a recent class at the Yoga Center of Minneapolis, I did a head count: 13 women and three men, including myself. This kind of ratio has been a normal experience for me. In fact, in the hundreds of yoga classes I have taken in studios across the Twin Cities metro area, there have been at least a few dozen times that I have been the only male participant. It wasn't surprising to learn that *Yoga Journal's* 2008 market study found that over 72 percent of American yoga practitioners are female. However, it did lead to me question why so many more women practice yoga than men.

Whereas North American yoga is predominantly practiced and led by women, the other spiritual community I am a part of – convert

American Zen Buddhism – has a different flavor. The average Zen center is fairly evenly divided in terms of gender (although female-led centers generally seem to attract more women than men). While the number of female teachers has greatly increased over the past two decades, the majority of teachers are still male. Furthermore, communities led by male teachers tend to have larger numbers of students in them. Generally, they are able to attract more financial support than those led by women, regardless of whether they are monastic or lay.

In a recent forum on women in Buddhism in the magazine *Buddhadharma,* Grace Schireson, founder of the Empty Nest Zendo Zen community, commented that "Zen hasn't developed the teachings to help women come forward as women." Later on in the forum, she spoke of archetypal image of a Zen master as the strong, silent male. Female Zen teachers are often held up to that standard, and frequently rejected as lesser than because of it. I have witnessed this very thing in my own Zen community, where a powerfully charismatic male teacher was replaced several years ago with a dynamic but unorthodox female teacher who continues to have her leadership skills questioned to this very day.

As a member of yoga's gender minority, who has practiced for over a decade and is now certified to teach, I have often wondered if there is more behind the gender divide, as well as the heavy focus on asana practice in North American yoga. While members of many spiritual and religious communities tend to emphasize the transcendent at the expense of the physical, the predominant theme amongst yoga practitioners appears to be the opposite. Whereas Zen students often get lost in their heads as they strive for enlightenment, the average yoga student is fixated on the appearance and general mechanics of their bodies. Given this contrast, I have wondered: Is it simply a coincidence that yoga has become a body-centric and overwhelmingly female practice, while the convert Zen community is more head-focused and male dominated? Or is there something more to it than that?

These are particularly interesting questions to consider given that modern Zen and yoga both emphasize body/mind integration. Many spiritual and religious paths focus on transcendent realms, suggesting that the body and the Earth itself are both corrupt, and that disassociating from them is an essential part of the practice. However, modern Zen and yoga both laud the present moment, teaching that people can awaken to their true nature by experiencing the now fully.

Near the end of his book *Light on Life*, B.K.S. Iyengar writes "My life's work has been to show how, even from humble beginnings, this is a path that can lead the dedicated practitioner to the integration of body, mind, and soul." Similar statements are easily found in many of the writings of modern Zen teachers. This leads me to wonder: If both of these paths are so focused on developing fully integrated humans, why do they both seem to be filled with students and even teachers who are trapped in one form of mind/body split or another?

In my view, the answer is twofold. First, the gender dynamics noted above point to differing manifestations of subtle and sometimes not so subtle sexism. Underlying this is a second issue: namely, that the loss of conscious connection with the rhythms of the natural world that pervades North American culture has infected our spiritual practices, including yoga and Zen, straight to the core. Consequently, healing our body/mind splits requires not only re-examining the role of gender, but also the ways in which we relate to, and interact with, the Earth.

Body Fixations/Mind Fixations

"You all are in a yoga teacher training program! You have to get this right!" My fellow yoga teacher trainees and I had just finished practicing, in painstaking detail, a section of a basic Sun Salutation for the fourth or fifth time. Scanning the class, it was obvious that most of my fellow students were just as exhausted as I was. At one point, I caught the eye of my closest neighbor, who quickly whispered, "I can't figure out what she wants." Halfway across the room, the teacher stood next to another student, watching her every move as she repeated what we all had just done. "Keep those elbows tucked! Don't just roll through *Chaturanga* on your way up!" She was clearly frustrated. At the time, I thought this was because of us. However, the longer I've sat with this experience, the more I have realized that she was mostly frustrated with herself. The aligning and flowing she had envisioned for these asanas wasn't manifesting. And in her mind, it was due to some failure on her part.

One of the notable elements of this experience was the way that our teacher pushed us to "get it right." Getting it right had everything to do with physical alignment and moving within that structure. It didn't matter if everyone was thinking constantly through the process, worried about making a mistake. It didn't matter much if our breath became ragged, or whether we followed the alignment our body was calling for on that particular day. No, the focus was on what our teacher felt was the "right" way to do Sun Salutations. That essentially meant focusing on bodily placement, and movement within that placement. She was so determined that we trainees "got it" that she was willing to push most of us past our limits, to the point where we were probably starting to check out mentally and emotionally in an effort to demonstrate the poses.

I've seen this in Zen communities as well, where students have "powered" themselves to sit endless hours of meditation, to the point where their bodies are riddled with chronic aches, pains, and injuries. Whereas yogis tend to check out of their minds and focus on their bodies, Zen practitioners often check out of their bodies and fixate on their minds. Sitting during meditation retreats with my entire body aching, until desperation led to peering around the room, I did my share of checking out on my body in the early years of my Zen practice. Seeing that nearly everyone else was still in half or full lotus posture, I would stay in half lotus myself, working to cut off the bodily sensations, and also often intellectualizing the pain as being "good for my practice."

More recently, I have begun to wonder how meditation retreats might be different if they were more regularly conducted outside, where people would be subject to shifting weather conditions, the movement of animals, and the smell of plants, among other things. Perhaps the emphasis on staying with physical pain, sometimes to the point of injury, is coming from the lack of natural stimuli one normally deals with when meditating outdoors. The nearly perfectly clean, enclosed meditation hall might offer far fewer potential distractions. But does it come at a cost?

A member of my Zen community recently spent nearly a year practicing at a monastery on the West Coast, only to return with a chronic knee injury that took several months to heal. He said that the practice atmosphere was kind of competitive, with a heavy emphasis on sitting meditation above all else. The way he described it, those who pushed themselves the hardest garnered the most respect in the community. Along these lines, it was common for students to sit up late into the night after formal meditation practice was over, staying in seated meditation postures regardless of the amount of pain they were experiencing.

Tibetan Buddhist teacher Reginald Ray, well known for his work on bringing body practices back into Buddhism, considers this issue endemic.

> My sense is that there is a very real problem amongst Western practitioners. We are attempting to practice meditation and to follow a spiritual practice in a disembodied state, and our practice is therefore doomed to failure. The full benefits and fruition of meditation cannot be experienced or enjoyed when we are not grounded in our bodies.

Ray's comments might be applied in the opposite direction for many yoga practitioners. If we aren't fully grounded in our minds while practicing, then the "full benefits and fruition" of the asana and other practices can't be experienced or enjoyed.

Fixing Students to "Get it right"

Not being grounded and present in our minds is just one example of the ways that the body/mind split can occur while practicing yoga. There are an assorted number of ways that teachers teach which add to the problem. For example, some are prone to giving overly powerful adjustments, which occasionally lead to student injuries. In a recent blog article, yoga teacher J. Brown reported the following incident:

> A friend of mine attended a large yoga event in NYC with a venerable teacher, considered to be a living "master." She was one of a very small percentage of the 600 participants to have the guru assist her in one of her poses, only to have her hamstring connector popped at his forceful hand. I remember seeing her several days later, and she was still in considerable pain.

Although I have never experienced something that extreme, I have had teachers shift my limbs too quickly in an attempt to create "proper" alignment, leaving me sore, and in a few cases, with limited mobility for multiple days following the class.

I have also encountered teachers who are overly reliant on physical and/or verbal adjustments, constantly feeling they need to "fix" the posture of their students. The woman in the example above from my teacher training, for example, frequently would spew anatomy cues in rapid fire, expecting us both to know the terms, and also quickly perform the adjustments she was calling for. Whenever someone fell far behind, she would stop in front of that student's mat, and use the student for an extended period of time as a demonstration model. While intending to provide a rigorous training, these incidences also demonstrated the teacher's propensity to lose track of time and failure to sense the limits of the students in her class. As such, many of us, myself included, desperately tried to keep up with most of the cues and adjustments in order to avoid having to spend what sometimes was upwards of eight to ten minutes being under the teachers' microscope in any given pose.

Along the same lines are the teachers who assume that there are narrow, fixed "right ways" to do each asana. One of the most challenging aspects of my yoga teacher training program was that one night you might work with a teacher that emphasized bent knees during forward folds, and the next night I would have a teacher arguing completely against that. On the positive side, this mixture of teacher instructions and views helped trainees to develop some flexibility. However, it was also the case that when someone taught poses rigidly, this benefit temporarily became a liability.

I remember practicing *Sirsasana* (Headstand) with two different teachers who helped me break through my fear of going upside down. They both focused on moving through the fear, getting up in a manner that was safe. But they also respected where my body strength was at on any given day. Not long after *Sirsasana* became a regular part of my practice, I encountered another teacher in the training program who was adamant that students should never kick their legs up from the floor to get into the pose. This is exactly what I had been doing. I was also, at the same time, using other poses to build core strength, so that I might eventually work my way into smoothly moving my legs from the floor into the air as advanced yogis do. After working with this teacher, I was afraid to do anything resembling headstand. I fully supported her desire to limit possible injuries, but for the next two or three weeks, I struggled to let go of her unnecessarily limiting view. Overall, it took over a month of practice before I was able to return to regularly doing *Sirsasana* as a part of my practice.

Some teachers also fail to recognize that physical differences in male and female bodies are important for certain poses. *Rajakapotasana* (King Pigeon Pose), for example, often looks and feels quite different for men and women due to the different shapes and sizes of their hipbones and overall pelvic region. Overall, such teaching creates another layer of inattention to the present moment for students. Instead of learning to respect and work with their bodies as they are today, students are given the message that yoga is about conforming to a narrow physical norm, one mostly driven by images of young, hyper-flexible, mostly female models. Teaching asana in a rigid, predetermined manner reflects a deep failure to honor the uniqueness of each person.

Gender Divides

Yoga marketing tends to focus on women in both respectful and stereotypical ways. From the fancy, feminine "yoga clothing" of companies like Lululemon, to the decidedly female-centric bent of publications like *Yoga Journal,* yoga is branded and sold as something that mostly women do. In fact, over the past nine years, *Yoga Journal* has had only a single male model on its covers. And while they have regularly featured male yoga teachers such as Jason Crandell and Roger Cole, the vast majority of articles and columns are written by women, and about female practitioners.

Gendered themes similarly prevail in the marketing of yoga by studios, gyms, and community centers. Yoga for weight loss. Yoga for tight abs, buns, and thighs. Flow yoga. Yoga for detox. These commonplace approaches generally appeal far more to the average woman than the average man. Indeed, with the exception of yoga classes geared towards athletes, and the occasional studio offering "Yoga for Guys" type classes, it's difficult for many men to find a hook in the advertising for, and writing about, yoga. At the same time, there is a strong emphasis placed on the physical practices of yoga, especially asana, while meditation and other spiritual elements are usually downplayed or marketed within a physical practice framework.

With the notable exceptions of Indra Devi and Geeta Iyengar, nearly all the masters who introduced yoga to the West were men. This shouldn't come as a surprise, given that until about a century ago, yoga was predominantly the practice of a small, elite group of Indian men. Some of the more well-known amongst those who introduced yoga to North America did, however, place a heavy emphasis on the physical practices, particularly asana. K. Pattabhi Jois and B.K.S. Iyengar, for example, both emphasized that the elevated levels of stress many Westerners have is antithetical to practicing the more subtle aspects of yoga. Given that their early Western students were a mixture of men and women, it's questionable to suggest that the focus on asana practice came from gender stereotypes. Jois originally designed his set of sequences primarily for teenage boys and young adult Indian men. And in Iyengar's case, the personal experience of healing from childhood tuberculosis played a large role in how he ended up structuring his yoga teaching.

Since I have a fair amount of experience in Iyengar-based practice, I will consider his approach a little more closely. In *Light on Life*, Iyengar writes "Technically speaking, true meditation in the yogic sense cannot be done by a person who is under stress or has a weak body." He goes on to explain that this "true meditation" isn't just "sitting quietly": it is a practice that leads us to "wisdom and awareness." One of the ways Iyengar attempts to get around what appears to be a separation of practices is to repeatedly speak of how meditation is contained within all the other limbs of practice, including asana. Indeed, recognizing the interconnectedness of all the yogic limbs is a large part of the reason he has put so much precision and intensity into teaching asana over the years.

Many students, however, simply can't experience that interconnectedness within the context of an asana-focused class. They are too busy taking in verbal cues, moving their bodies, and responding to physical adjustments. Furthermore, the entire way in which the practice is often framed – as being about exercise, health, or even wellness – adds another blockage. Even as someone who has long studied the spiritual teachings of yoga, my own experience in the classroom tends to be mixed. Sometimes, everything will settle enough to allow my mind to focus on the present. But other times, I am either trying to figure out what is being taught, or my mind is lost in thinking.

This mixed bag experience is commonplace. And in and of itself, is not an issue at all. Yoga teacher Stephen Cope once wrote that "alienation from the self is the entire focus of yoga philosophy." In other words, it makes sense that sometimes you will be fully present, and other times you will check out somehow. However, I'm not convinced that the mind/body splitting we are seeing in yoga is only about the regular alienation each of us has with our true selves.

Consider the work of Geeta Iyengar, the daughter of B.K.S. Iyengar. Recognizing that the practice she learned was missing a restorative element, she pioneered methods of shifting asana poses into a more passive, restful experience, using bolsters, props and blankets. Although "restorative yoga" isn't a gender-specific practice, it can been seen as a counterbalance to the active, some might say "masculine," quality of many asana poses in particular, as well as the practice of asana as a whole. In addition, the majority of her teaching and writing has focused on yoga and women. Again, recognizing that something was missing in traditional yoga, she's designed practices entirely focused on the unique needs of the female body. This includes sequences for menstruation, pregnancy, postpartum depression, and menopause, as well as posture alignment work based on common differences between male and female bodies.

As more and more female Zen students have risen in the ranks and become either teachers or senior-level students, there have been similar efforts to address some of the patriarchal norms of the practice. Some elements of my home *Sangha*, Clouds in Water Zen Center, display these efforts firsthand. While many American Zen communities are almost solely focused on formal meditation practice and textual study, Clouds has also offered, from its early days, a broad-based youth program in an effort to serve those with children. We have regular classes focused on integrating Buddhist teachings into our daily lives. More recently, we have developed member support networks for those who are sick or in crisis, as well as a group for those wishing to actively engage in the community and work together on various social issues. Furthermore, we have adopted a regular practice of chanting the names of female ancestors from a lineage compiled by feminist Buddhist scholars in the past decade or so. And we have added female figures to our community altars, including a Kwan Yin figure (representing boundless compassion) in our main meditation hall. While none of these practices are unique to Clouds in Water, they do represent a departure from models that were brought to North America and the Zen communities that developed here during most of the 20th century.

While what might be called a "feminization" of practice has occurred in both North American yoga and Zen, neither seem fully liberated from sexist elements. The often superficial marketing of yoga, appealing to stereotypical images of "beautiful," young female bodies, as well as the continued heavy reliance on physical postures developed by and for men, are just two examples in the North American yoga world. Whereas in Zen, the continued heavy reliance on monastic approaches that were tailored to young and middle-aged men, as well as the struggle women teachers continue to have in gaining the kind of recognition and consideration that some of their male counterparts do, are problematic areas of concern. However, in both cases, something else also appears to be at play. Something much broader, and yet which has long been tied to the marginalization and oppression of women. Namely, our common tendency as North Americans to live in a state that feels divorced from the Earth itself.

Divided from the Planet

I have practiced yoga in some beautiful, almost immaculate studio spaces over the past several years. And I've often felt gratitude for the care that's put in to the upkeep of these places. The same thing can be said of Clouds in Water Zen Center, with its pristine meditation halls and gathering spaces. At the same time, however, it's become increasingly clear to me how such practice environments reflect the ways in which so many of us are split off from the very earth we are made of. The nearly pristine floors. The rationally ordered props and altars. The air conditioning in the summer. The centralized heating in the winter. The severe lack of wildness.

Throughout most of its history, yoga has been practiced either outdoors or within simple structures designed to protect people from the extremes. And whereas Zen has been long practiced in monastic buildings, monks and nuns traditionally spent much of their day outdoors, gathering materials for cooking, traversing the villages, and even meditating along the roads and in the fields. Something of the depth of wisdom is lost, or difficult to locate anyway, when the practices are cloistered in today's tamed environments. It's easy to forget, for example, that the Buddha became enlightened while sitting at the foot of a tree. Or that many of the postures we practice in yoga were directly taken from observations of animals, plants, and elements of the Earth.

Simply put, humans have become alienated from our own planet. It's notable that yogic practices developed around the time this alienation seemed to be forming. Buddhism came later, with Zen forming as an offshoot some 1,500-1,600 years ago. For all the benefits we have received from agriculture, as well as the development of cities and societies, much has also been lost. The litany of abuse people have unleashed upon the earth, especially in recent centuries, is clearly a sign of deep disconnections, so deep that for some that they might destroy the entire planet in the long term, if it meant big material profits in the short term.

Probably from the beginning, this disconnection has been tied to the oppression of women. Ecofeminist Susan Griffin suggests that we have been living in a "bifurcated system" where the natural world has been turned into something in need of "mastery and domination." In this system, emotions, vulnerability, and tenderness have become "forms of submission." In the process, women have been socialized "to be more connected with the body than are men, for whom this connection represents a threat." Even the very ways in which we conceptualize and relate to the Earth have been greatly distorted, and used "to justify the social construction of gender."

Perhaps those early yogis and Buddhists intuitively felt some of this separation occurring. Maybe they were offering a way for people to re-pattern themselves amidst the unhealthy current around them. Given that yoga, and to a somewhat lesser degree Buddhism, remained primarily the domain of men of elite social status until recent centuries, however, it's obvious that some of that separation had already penetrated quite deeply.

Although I didn't have the intention in the beginning, I now prac-tice yoga and Zen together out of a deep longing to heal this bifurcated system. In the end, this system oppresses us all. It limits not only our spiritual capacity, but our everyday lives in general.

In and of themselves, an overzealous focus on body alignment or over-reliance on marathon meditation sessions might be chalked up to individual character flaws. However, when placed in the stew of our deeply misguided, collective relationship with the planet, it's hard not to see the bigger picture. How we are exhibiting mind/body splits in-dividually is directly correlated to how the vast majority of our society is divided from the very ground upon which we stand, and the very air we breathe. We are divided not only within ourselves, but also from the original great body of Mother Earth as well.

Mind/Body Bridge Practices

It's vital that yoga, Zen, and other spiritual communities in North America diversify their practices to foster more integration, both within ourselves and with our natural world. Here, I present some suggestions for practices that might help us address the mind/body splits occurring in the North American yoga community in particular. I consider them bridge practices that could also be applied by Zen students, or others working on mind/body integration. May they be seeds for further conversation and exploration.

Emphasize the Yamas and Niyamas: One strength of Clouds in Water Zen Center is a strong emphasis on the Buddhist precepts: our ethical teachings. They help ground our practice in everyday experience, and give students an opportunity for reflection as well as ways to approach aspects of their lives differently. Yoga teachers could teach directly about *Ahimsa* (non-violence), for example, in more vigorous classes to help reduce the amount of injuries people experience. In addition, *Ahimsa* can be applied in any class to the ways we think, helping students to recognize the negative self-talk and other violence that often floats through our minds during yoga classes (and our lives in general).

Another useful *Yama* is *Aparigraha* (non-possessiveness). This could be a direct antidote to the heavy achievement and acquisition drives that are built into our society, and plague so many of us. Simply emphasizing that there's nothing to gain, and that yoga isn't about achieving something like "perfect poses" is one way to do this. In addition to *Ahimsa* and *Aparigraha,* most of the other *Yamas* and *Niyamas* could be applied in ways that would aid students in reintegrating the mind-body. Even *Ishvarapranidhana* (surrender to God) can be incorporated into any class by focusing on surrendering and letting go.

Practice outdoors more often: I have practiced yoga and meditation in parks, along rivers and lakes, even in the middle of a few forests. I distinctly remember the joy I felt doing Sun Salutations under the midday sun in a field of dandelions. Flowing between Downward Facing Dog and Upward Facing Dog in particular, I recall how open my senses were, how every breath was like drinking the world. There have been some amazing street yoga programs that have developed in cities around the U.S. and Canada in recent years, including Gorilla Yogis here in Minneapolis-St. Paul. In addition, more teachers are taking classes into the parks, at least during the summer — a sign that the limitations of indoor spaces are being recognized.

Experience Dark Meditation: Awhile back, I listened to a Sounds True podcast interview with Buddhist teacher Reggie Ray, in which he described a practice called Dark Meditation. Essentially, it's a practice of going into complete darkness and staying with whatever comes up. After the interview, I went into my bathroom, covered up all the entry points of light, and sat for an hour in the darkness. It was a very interesting experience. You know your body is there, the bathtub is there, the toilet is there – but you can't see any of it. It doesn't take long before you start feeling disoriented – not in an awful way, but in a "what is this experience" kind of way.

The natural curiosity each of us has, but which often is blocked, comes forth rather easily from the darkness. And because you can't see your body, it requires you to reorient yourself to what you are experiencing. This could be an excellent re-patterning practice for those who are highly attached to how they look and appear physically in the world.

Try Yoga Nidra: Otherwise known as the yoga of sleep, *Yoga Nidra* is part deep relaxation practice and part meditation. Although it can be done in any position, it's often conducted while lying down and supported by blankets and/or bolsters. On the surface, it appears to be very similar to *Savasana* (Corpse Pose), and it is true that both have a focus on deep relaxation. However, whereas *Savasana* is mostly about letting go, *Yoga Nidra* tends to be a more active, directed practice. Part of the promise of *Nidra* rests in the frequent cues to locate your attention in places all over the body. As you scan your body, and take in whatever sensations arise, there is a natural re-embodying that occurs. In addition, the deeper the practice goes, the more it's designed to help you tap into your true self through images, emotional releases, and energy alignment.

Every session includes a call to an intention, something you begin and end the practice with – and which can aid in redirecting one's life towards a truer expression.

Reconciling Ourselves and the World

In the end, yoga and Zen are both paths of healing and of awakening to our true nature. Over the centuries, they have evolved in response to the needs of the people of that given time period. Today, more and more people are sensing something is off in their lives and in the world, and are making an effort to right the course. This is wonderful. However, it is important to develop a mind of experimentation, recognizing not only that gender differences need be taken into consideration, but also that righting our collective relationship with the Earth must be moved to the forefront. The times are calling us to both reconcile ourselves, and reunify with the Earth itself. May we use our practices as a laboratory of healing, so that we may awaken to the fullest expression of our lives.

5

Starved for Connection:
Healing Anorexia Through Yoga

Chelsea Roff

There is no greater agony than bearing an untold story inside of you.
—Maya Angelou

The Day a Part of My Brain Died

Fifteen-year-olds aren't supposed to have strokes. At least that's what I thought. I try not to think about it too much. Even now, I only have bits and pieces; shards of memories that somehow remained intact even through the trauma my brain endured that day.

The morning started out like any other. I woke up around eight a.m., hobbled into the bathroom, and emptied my bladder mindlessly into the commode. This routine — piss and weigh, first thing in the

morning – had become almost involuntary, drilled into my neural archi-
tecture through repetition over the past several years. Pulling the scale
out from the cabinet beneath the sink, I placed one foot on and then the
other. Fifty-eight pounds.

My little sister, Avery – 14 at the time – was getting ready to leave
for the grocery store when I asked if I could come along. She shook her
head no, told me she was perfectly capable of buying what was on the
list and didn't need my help to make selections. I told her I needed to
go, needed to get out of the house and get some fresh air. I told her that
I felt like a caged animal. She rolled her eyes, but agreed.

I was notorious for prolonging grocery trips from minutes to hours
upon end. I would roam the aisles slowly and methodically, picking up
items I would never dream of eating just to read the ingredients. The
produce section was my favorite. I loved to hold each little fruit in my
hand, squeeze and caress apples with wanton desire until I found just
the right one. I read labels like they were romance novels, scanning the
nutritional information as if reading about vitamins and minerals would
transfuse them into my body. I was obsessed with food. I just didn't like
eating it.

I glanced in the bathroom mirror to check my hair on my way up-
stairs to get my wallet. Pause. I normally didn't look – really look – at
myself when I gazed in mirrors, but something made me do a double
take that morning. I involuntarily gasped when I met eyes with the
haunting reflection peering back at me. I truly didn't recognize my
own face in the mirror. That skeletal ghost . . . I didn't believe it. It
wasn't me.

I turned away and headed toward the stairs to make my ascent. I
climbed stairs like an old woman now; it took so much effort just to
raise my leg that 10 inches for each step. I placed one foot slowly ahead
of the other, gripping the handrail for dear life. I think I'd reached the
fourth step when my breath caught in my throat. I literally couldn't get
enough oxygen in my lungs. I paused, collapsed down onto the stairs,

buried my head in my hands. Inhale. Exhale. Inhale. Exhale. Must get breath.

My sister cleared her throat from the bottom of the stairwell a few steps down. "You want me to get it for you?"

"I . . . I can't make it up." My voice was barely a whisper.

The next clear memory I have is walking into Whole Foods with my sister, wallet in my back pocket and grocery list in hand. Avery suggested I sit in one of the motorized grocery carts, reminding me that the doctor had insisted I stay on bed rest until I gained weight. I sneered. There was no way I was sitting my bony ass down in a cart for handicapped people. I was invincible. I wanted to walk, and so I did.

I was wandering down an aisle in search of the lowest-calorie marinara sauce when I began to lose my vision: first just the peripheral edges, and then black spots in the center field. Within another minute my auditory sense began to slip away. All I could hear was a weird buzzing tone in my right ear, as if there had been a sudden change of air pressure in the room. A few moments later I collapsed.

The next thing I remember – it could have been a day, maybe a week later – is sitting in a wheelchair at Children's Medical Center in Dallas. A therapist was squeezing my hand, tears brimming in her eyes. Muffled voices. "She's lucky to be alive."

From the Valley of Death

After a five-year long battle with anorexia nervosa, my body had reached its breaking point. When I arrived at Children's nearly every system in my body was shutting down. All four valves in my heart were leaking. My skin was yellow from liver failure. I hadn't take a shit in over a month. I was dying.

The first emotion I remember is rage. It was a violent, fire-in-your-veins, so angry-you-could-kill-someone kind of rage. I wanted out. I wanted the pain to be over. I wanted to die. I was mad at myself for not having the courage to just do it quickly, angry at the hospital staff for thwarting my masked attempt. I was convinced that I was "meant to" endure this, that my long drawn-out starving to death would prove my willpower to God. In the days prior to my stroke, I'd had vivid hallucinations – of Jesus on a wooden cross outside my bedroom window and a satanic figure sneaking up under my bedroom covers to suffocate me at night. I thought I was meant to be a martyr.

I thought God wanted me to die.

As the fury subsided, delirium set in. I became confused, defiant, and completely irrational. I told the other patients that my Mom would be there to pick me up and take me home any day now. I argued with the doctors that they couldn't possibly keep me overnight, because we didn't have insurance or money to pay. When a cardiologist told me she wasn't sure if I'd live another week, I told her she was full of shit. I hid the food they were trying to make me eat in my underwear, in flowerpots, even in my cheeks like a chipmunk – convinced no one would notice. I didn't want to get better. I was convinced nothing was wrong.

I remember having nurses turn me over in the middle of the night to tend to the bed sores on my behind, places where the skin was so thin that my tail bone was starting to protrude through the flesh. I remember waking up to discover I'd wet the bed nearly every morning for the first three months I was there. I was ashamed, disgusted. I'd lost control of the muscles in my bladder; I was like an infant all over again. I remember shooting a nurse the bird when she told me I couldn't walk, only to fall to pieces on the floor when I angrily pushed the wheelchair away to give it a try.

Unbeknownst to me at the time, my arrival at the hospital had launched an investigation by Child Protective Services back at my home in Austin. The caseworkers deemed my mother an "unfit parent," and my sister and I were placed under custodianship of the State. My care was left to the doctors and nurses at Children's, while my sister was officially placed in foster care and sent to live with our godparents. My mother, herself an alcoholic and anorexic, had literally drank herself into oblivion.

I spent the next 16 months of my life in that hospital. I completed my junior and senior years of high school through a distance education program, talked my way through hundreds of hours of individual and group therapy, and slowly, painfully worked to bring my body and mind back to life.

My main doctor, Dr. Wooten, became very much like a father to me. At first I hated him. He held a firm line when it came to my medical treatment, and within my first week at the hospital I'd branded him a control freak and male chauvinist. I demanded a new (female) doctor and told my caseworker that it would be traumatic for me to continue working with him. He was the first person in my life to set boundaries with me and stick to them, and I hated him for it. No, you can't hide food in your underpants. No, you can't get out of your wheelchair. I'm going to take care of you, whether you like it or not.

Over the next few months, as my body grew accustomed to having nourishment again, my temperament and personality began to change. I became quieter, more submissive, more trusting of the staff in charge of my care. I soon found that despite his seemingly arrogant exterior, Dr. Wooten was a gentle, incredibly compassionate person inside. He said "no" to me because he cared. For my first Halloween in the hospital, I had the other staff members help me dress up like him for my costume. I wore his clean white coat, black-rimmed glasses, hung a stethoscope around my neck. In the morning when he showed up for rounds, I offered my hand and in a very low voice said, "Please, call me Tyler." He laughed and laughed. "You, Miss Chelsea," he said. "You are something else."

One night, one of my nurses, Miss Connie, pulled me gingerly from my wheelchair and into her lap in a chair next to the window. Her curly blonde locks brushed my sunken cheekbones as we gazed out at the distant sunset together. "Just keep your eyes on that horizon, honey." she said. "You're going to survive this."

Dr. Wooten, Miss Connie, and the other staff members at Children's became like a family to me. They didn't just show up and do their jobs; they took a stake in my healing, going above and beyond what is required of any medical professional. They inspired my tired spirit to hang in there in the face of extreme, debilitating heartbreak. They reminded me of why I ultimately chose to live . . . because I wanted to connect, to love.

When Medicaid finally pulled the plug on funding for my treatment almost a year and a half later, I was unrecognizable from the day I'd walked in. I'd gained nearly forty pounds, and the feisty, fiercely independent spirit I'd been known for as a child was on her way back in (close to) full force. Although I was still significantly underweight and terrified to leave the security of the hospital, my medical team still managed to convince the state to grant me emancipation. At 17, I re-entered the "real world" as a legally recognized adult.

Dr. Wooten helped me make arrangements to move into a garage apartment with a close family friend who lived close to the hospital. I also managed to get a job at a local Starbucks earning just above minimum wage. By the grace of who-knows-what, the psychologist who had been the one to squeeze my hand that first day at Children's offered me nearly free weekly therapy. I was lucky. I was blessed. I had enough resources to begin to put the fragments of my broken life back together.

The Hook and The Sutra

Several months after my discharge, I took my first yoga class. Looking back on it now, I still find it hard to believe that I managed to find my way into that studio, with that teacher, at that moment in my life. I mean, really, what was I thinking – a recovering anorexic, barely able to feed herself – trying out a yoga class marketed to women wanting to lose weight?

I wish I could say I went to yoga because I had some inkling that it would offer me something deeper, because there was an inexplicable spiritual tug, because I was looking to reconnect with my body and begin the real process of healing. Quite the contrary. My motivations for trying yoga were almost entirely pathological. I was looking for a quick fix, a sneaky way to burn calories without arousing the suspicions of my treatment team.

After only a few months away from the hospital, I was slipping back into old, self-destructive behaviors. I was emotionally overwhelmed, lonely, and I felt like an alien in my new larger body. Bicycling and running were not an option because of lingering heart issues . . . but yoga? Well, yoga got the thumbs up from the therapist. If it had not been a roundabout way to burn calories, I never would have walked into that class.

So I did what anyone would do . . . I Googled "yoga studio" with my zip code and found a small studio located within just a few miles of my house. The website was simple and welcoming, the introductory offer so cheap that I couldn't pull the "I can't afford it" excuse. And when I saw the words "Power Yoga" on the schedule, I was sold. It sounded like one of my old aerobic classes at the gym. This would be my kind of yoga.

That evening I cloaked myself in an oversized sweatshirt and baggy pants that just barely hung onto my pointy little hip bones. I had to hide the body I felt had gotten too big to tolerate. I walked into that studio feeling anxious and suspicious, praying no one would notice me. The first thing I saw when I walked in was a big, fat Ganesh statue by the door . . . *Oh, hell no,* I thought. I almost turned around right then.

It seems almost laughable now, but my first yoga teacher was this big, voluptuous black woman — one fucking powerhouse of a human being. She emanated strength, beauty, and grace like no one I'd ever met before. Her voice was loud and bellowing as she sung out "Well, hello there!" from inside the practice room, her feet thumped with confidence as she trotted toward me on the hardwood floor. I was completely mesmerized by the way she carried herself, how she softly but powerfully filled the space.

For years, I'd been starving myself in order to take up *less* space in the world. I'd been taught by my own mother that strength came from mastering the wild whims of the body, controlling your instinctual urges, from proving you were stronger than others through stubborn will. And here was Diana, a woman who could hold all 200 pounds of her sweet self up in Handstand with ease. A woman who inhabited her life-given figure with confidence, compassion, and fierce femininity.

Diana not only stood counter to the traditional image of yoga I'd seen plastered on fitness magazines, but looking back I realize that she was hilariously non-traditional in the way she led class. I think it was during my second class – we were just about to start sun salutations – when she suddenly ran over to the stereo and turned the music up to full volume. Out of the speakers I hear none other than The Artist Formerly Known as Prince singing, "Go 'head now! Go Chelsea!" Diana danced over to me, a huge smile on her face, and sang, "Go 'head now! Go, Chelsea!" as I stepped back into *Chaturanga* – my cheeks flushed beet-red.

I burst out laughing. Fits of giggles rippled through my entire body; my belly shook uncontrollably with convulsions. I don't think I'd experienced myself so fully embodied in such raw, unadulterated joy since . . . well, I'm not sure I'd ever felt something like that before. Something in me broke open. Diana had seen me, celebrated my mere existence in the room, and something about the mix of shy embarrassment, relief, and gratitude that simple act of "seeing" evoked allowed an emotion that had been lying dormant in the pit of my stomach for years to release. The floodgates were open. Joy poured out.

That was my initiation into the practice of yoga. While I don't think I realized it at the time, Diana had just imparted a thread of wisdom — a *Sutra,* if you will — far more valuable than any 3000-year-old yogic text ever could. This is what I wrote in my journal that night:

> *Your body is not your enemy. Quite the contrary, that beautiful body of yours can be a conduit for joy and ecstasy, if only you will let yourself be seen and connect with others.*

I was hooked.

Subtle Transformation

Over the next year, I began practicing regularly at Diana's studio. At first it was just a few times a week, but soon I was an everyday practitioner. Diana offered me unlimited yoga classes in exchange for cleaning her studio twice a week. God bless her. I would never have been able to afford a regular studio's prices. Outside of work and school (I had enrolled in a local university by this time), yoga became the central focus of my life. I started setting my schedule to fit my yoga classes, rather than the other way around. I devoured books, podcasts, blogs, and documentaries about yoga and related philosophies. I wanted to get it, to understand it, to figure out what it was about the practice that felt so damn special.

The truth, however, is that no degree of intellectual understanding could explain (or justify) the experiences I was having on my mat. Yoga, in the biggest sense of the word, was subtly shifting the way I related to my body and my self. Contrary to the popularized New Age notions of "transformation," the shifts I experienced didn't happen in some pivotal, light-up-the-sky ah-ha moment. In fact, I think for the most part I was relatively unaware that yoga was "transforming" me at all. I just knew I wanted to be in that room, that I wanted to practice. It's only been with time and distance that I've been able to look back and pinpoint some of the elements of my yoga experience that were crucial to my recovery: *connection to body, peace and relaxation, intimacy and pleasure,* and *embodied trauma work.*

Connection to Body: When I first started practicing, I simply could not fathom the idea of "listening to your body." A teacher would give an instruction like "let your body be your guide" or "feel your way into the pose," and I would just roll my eyes. Let your body be your guide? What the heck was that supposed to mean? There was a right way and a wrong way, either your foot was in the right position or it wasn't. I had very little awareness of the soft utterances my body made when it was overstretched or the way that an inhale would catch in my throat if I pushed too far. I dismissed half of what was said each class as meaningless mumbo-jumbo, some blissed-out yoga teacher's way of "fluffifying" her prose.

But over time, I – inadvertently, mind you – began to connect with the somatic experience I was having on my mat. It wasn't a purposeful, deliberate process . . . it simply happened, almost unconsciously, sometimes with the help of an observant and intuitive teacher. One day, we were lying on the ground in a spinal twist when my belly let out a huge grumble. I didn't notice. I had taught myself for years to ignore the sensations and sounds of my body. But Diana, who was just a few feet away, smiled and said, "Hmmmm. Someone must be hungry." I was stunned. Hunger? That's what hunger felt like?

So much of my eating disorder had been about denying and eliminating my sensual experience. I wasn't hungry. I didn't need food. I refused to be a slave to my body. And here was this practice, re-introducing me to my feet, to the sensations in my belly, to the ecstasy of releasing long-held tension in the tiny muscles of my neck and back. Slowly and without my awareness, yoga rebuilt the neural bridges that connected my brain to my body, my mind to my physical reality. I learned to be with my body, rather than run away from its sensations.

Peace and Relaxation: There were several types of classes on the schedule at Diana's studio, but I quickly learned that anything labeled "Gentle," "Restorative," or "Hatha" were *not* for me. I loved the dynamic flow of Sun Salutations, the challenge of contorting my body into some-times painful and exhausting positions, the perfectionistic specificity embedded in the Ashtanga sequence. I always struggled in the latter half of class. As soon as my butt hit the ground, I felt a boiling angst well up within me, shooting daggers of judgment at whoever was leading the class. I was there to exercise, to burn some calories – not to sit and relax.

But the practice was patient with me. Yoga provided just enough physical exertion to keep me hooked, while slipping in the deep doses of release and relaxation I really needed. After a few weeks of finger-tap-ping during *Savasana,* squirming in Half Pigeons, and resisting those so-deep-you-can-feel-your-belly forward folds, I finally gave in. Like a starving child tasting real and nourishing food for the first time, I de-voured the silence and space created by the more "passive" asanas. I learned to relax and allow myself to experience the pleasure of my body.

Intimacy and Pleasure: I once heard Bryan Kest say, "Yoga is like public masturbation. It's about touching and pleasuring yourself." Had that sentiment been shared with me when I first started practicing, I would have went running for the door. I was terrified of my own sexu-ality. I refused to look at myself in the mirror, denied my femininity, rejected pleasure as something that was dirty, shameful, even dangerous. Yoga began to change that.

The sweet, sensual experience of touching and stretching my own body created the foundation necessary for an intimate relationship with myself. I learned to notice what felt good, what felt bad; I became aware of my reactions in the face discomfort, my relationship to pleasure. Very simply, yoga held up a mirror to my internal experience. For years, I'd been ignoring the sensations in my body. The practice was like coming home to myself.

As my inhibitions fell away and repetition built confidence, I no-ticed a woman (not girl) I'd never met before beginning to emerge. She was strong, sensual, even seductive. There were days on the mat I felt beautiful, uninhibited, free to move in my natural grace and strength. There was something about getting that engrossed in movement – skin rubbing on skin, sweat dripping down my chest, exhales stroking my upper lip – that allowed me to experience my body as a vessel for the woman I was becoming. No amount of "positive self-talk" or "cognitive reframing" would ever bring me to a place of such self-love.

Embodied Trauma Work: Finally, yoga provided an opportunity to explore and heal the trauma that up until that point had not reached consciousness – despite the fact that I'd been in therapy since I was twelve. As the layers of tension began to fall away, certain asanas evoked memories, visceral experiences, and sensations that I had no words for. My mat provided a safe space for me to simply let the tears flow rather than having to weave a story around them.

Yoga provided an opportunity to explore my past through my body. There were some heartbreaks I simply could not talk about in therapy, experiences that at the time felt so shameful and intolerable that I simply didn't have the capacity to express them in words. I can't count the number of times I went to a yoga class directly after an appointment – exhausted, disheveled, and frustrated with myself for not being able to describe what was happening inside of me. Then, after 90 minutes of yoga, the slate was wiped clean. I moved through whatever was coming up rather than letting myself fester in it. I learned to be with emotions and memories that I'd almost killed myself trying to stave off.

I don't know if I would be here today if I had not discovered this practice. Treatment, in many ways, had put a Band-Aid on the deep psychological wounds I was embodying. In the hospital, I had been taught to eat when I wasn't hungry, separate my thoughts from my feelings, to stop looking in the mirror altogether so I wouldn't sabotage myself. To survive, I *had* to disconnect from my body and my emotions, simply because I didn't have the resources to cope with them. Yoga brought me back.

But while the practice played an integral role in my healing, I don't want to suggest yoga is some type of panacea for people struggling with eating disorders. Quite the contrary, I think yoga can be a double-edged sword for any of us — especially those grappling with addiction, grief, or a stressful life event. Trauma, whether in the form of sexual abuse, divorce, the loss of a loved one, or simply moving to a new city, will inevitably alter the way we approach yoga and our lives. If we're feeling vulnerable, hurt, desperate, or overwhelmed, yoga can easily become a means to numb or even injure ourselves.

As someone who was barely on the cusp of recovery, you better believe I grabbed it. Soon enough, yoga became just as harmful as it had been healing.

Medicine and Malady

I was lying in bed late one Friday night when my younger sister called me, panic in her voice: *"I can't find mom. I came over to the house to check on her, and there's blood all over the place. Her car's gone. Chelsea, it looks like a murder scene."*

After two days of calling nearly every hospital in Austin, I found my mother at the Williamson County Jail. After a little more investigation, I learned that a police officer had found her unconscious at a local gas station. She'd apparently driven there after falling down the stairs at her house and collapsed in a pool of blood. I drove down to Austin the next day to bail her out, and, where my mother had once been, found a glazy-eyed, wheelchair-bound woman who didn't recognize me. She stared blankly at me through the two inches of glass that separated us, drool seeping from the corners of her pursed lips. She was confused, delirious . . . and probably, as I had once been, lucky to be alive.

My mother was later diagnosed with Wernicke's Syndrome, a form of alcohol-induced dementia that left her with the cognitive capacities of a ten-year-old. It was another three months before she was released from jail. During this time, I tried to convince my sister (who was living the wild life of an unbridled teenager) to come and live with me in Dallas. At just 20 years old, I found myself standing in an oversized business suit before a judge at the county courthouse, pleading for custody of both of them. I thought I could handle it. I was wrong.

Ultimately, the judge gave me legal custody of my mother but decided I was too young to take legal responsibility for my little sister. With my aunt's help, I placed my mother in a group home for people with mental disorders in Austin. Eventually, I brought my sister to Dallas to live with the same family friend I'd stayed with after I left the hospital.

Despite the calm, collected exterior I exuded to the people around me, inside I was falling apart. I simply did not have the resources to cope with what was happening. I felt like my mother had committed suicide; gone was the woman I'd known as a child. While she hadn't been perfect, at least she'd been my mother. Now, there was just this alien, this decoy, this pitiful shell of a human being who didn't even recognize me most of the time. I was angry and hurt, but I refused to acknowledge it. I went into caretaker mode, handled my relationship with her as if she were a stranger. I had to be strong.

But inside, I was still a child. And though I would never have admitted it to anyone, I wanted my Mommy back. I felt alone and abandoned. I wondered if my illness had caused her decline. I felt like someone had literally reached inside me and torn my heart out.

As the emotions intensified, so did my yoga practice. I was desperate for something to numb my misery, and my mat provided the perfect opportunity to work my body and mind into exhausted oblivion. Yoga became a place to run and hide, to arouse enough physical sensation that I couldn't feel anything else. I would hold my leg up in *Padagusthasana* until my entire body quaked; I'd clench my jaw until all I could think about was the pain. I kept my mind busy with the steady, mind-numbing movement of Vinyasa. And when *Savasana* came, I would count ceiling tiles, praying not to feel.

To my teachers, fellow students, and even my therapist, I was just one really dedicated practitioner. In reality, I was more like a crack addict . . . desperate for another fix. I came to get high, to hide from the pain, to shrink my body again. Over the next three months, my twice-a-day Vinyasa habit helped me shed almost 15 pounds from my already underweight frame.

As my body started to disintegrate, so did my mental and emotional state. One of the interesting biological effects of under-nutrition, whether it be from over-exercising or inadequate food intake, is that semi-starvation causes you to become more anxious, self-critical, and (ironically) obsessed with food. This is actually a clinically-studied phenomenon. An infamous study called the Minnesota Starvation Experiment revealed that when people eat less than their caloric requirements for extended periods of time, they become socially isolated, self-destructive, and obsessive compulsive. My body was in starvation mode again. I ate enough to keep my weight just above my "danger zone," but the psychological effects of my eating disorder were back.

It is difficult to acknowledge now, but yoga had become just another tool I used to starve myself. I'm not speaking metaphorically; I had it down to a science. I actually timed my yoga practices to be right when a meal should have been, knowing the physical exertion would suppress my body's hunger signals. I started the day with an Ashtanga practice, red-eyed my way through the day with coffee, had a large meal at three, and fell into a coma-esque slumber by four. When I awoke, I'd practice again and wait until two in the morning when "I felt hungry again" to eat. I hid my pain and my addiction under the mask of a spiritual practice. In reality, I was depressed, dysfunctional, and too proud to ask for help.

Returning to Love

By March 2010, my weight had dropped so low that I was getting comments from strangers about how frail I looked – an experience all too reminiscent of the days and months leading up to my stroke. Oddly enough, I was also receiving praise from fellow yoga students about my emaciated appearance. "How did you get your arms so toned?" one woman asked me before class, reaching out to pinch my bicep. I recoiled. "Starve yourself," I thought in my head. But to her, I just said: "Gotta love those *Chaturangas.*"

My starve-eat-sleep-repeat cycle was also getting in the way of my studies. I was falling asleep in class, skipping study groups to go to yoga, hiding in the bathroom at lunch because I was afraid to eat in front of people. I pushed away the few people in my life that might have intervened at that point, and in therapy I was talking about everything *but* my food and exercise habits. I convinced myself that nothing was wrong. I couldn't acknowledge my own needs and vulnerability. I was right back on the road to hell.

One night, after waking up from another one of my hypoglycemic slumbers, I decided to take a late night class at a local Power Yoga studio called The Yoga Project. I had been once before but hadn't gone back because the heated practice room irritated my nervous system. That night though, I didn't care. I wanted to burn.

By some incredibly fortunate turn of fate, I ended up being the only student who showed up for the class. Rather than scoot me out the door per the studio's one-student cancellation policy, the teacher – Stacy – sat on the ground and talked with me. She asked me why I'd come to such a late night yoga class. I told her I wasn't sleeping well. She asked me if I was depressed. I told her I wasn't sure. We talked about everything from dreams of travel to the meaning of compassion. I couldn't put my finger on what it was, but I felt inexplicably close to Stacy – like I'd known her my entire life.

It was nearly 9-o'clock and we'd been talking for almost an hour. Stacy asked if I would come back for class the next morning. I hesitated. I never went to bed before 3 a.m., and I didn't get up before ten o'clock. I told her I wasn't sure. She smiled. "Leave your mat here," she said. "You'll come."

Despite all my reservations, I did.

The next morning I walked in snotty-eyed and grumpy, and there was Stacy, wide awake and chipper as hell. She embraced me. "I knew you'd come!" she said. As we settled into the first Child's Pose of the class, Stacy placed a firm but gentle hand on my low back. I nearly cried. I felt welcome. I felt seen. And as cheesy as it may sound, I felt loved.

Over the next few months, I completely immersed myself in the community at The Yoga Project. It had barely been four weeks when Stacy offered me a front desk job, and I found myself with something to do during the day other than starve, eat, and sleep. I made friends with the other staff members, attended every single weekend workshop and training, and put all my front desk salaries toward enlisting in their 200-hour teacher program. I became part of a close-knit and deeply supportive community at The Yoga Project. I finally had an identity beyond "that girl with an eating disorder."

Almost two years after I'd left my nest at Children's, I found myself once again being nurtured by a network of support – a family that I'd chosen and created for myself. Stacy became like a mother to me, the other teachers like older siblings I'd never had. I eventually opened up about the fact that I'd struggled with an eating disorder, a truth I'd been desperately trying to hide from everyone in my life. I was ashamed of having had anorexia, and terrified that if people knew they might think I was shallow, childish, or just not strong enough to take care of myself. The reaction, however, was one of only love and support. All of a sudden I had people inviting me over for dinner, bringing me burritos during my work shifts, asking, "Do you need anything? Can I help?"

One teacher, Kristi, and I became especially close friends. We started going to a bagel shop every morning after class, and even on the days I didn't want to eat . . . I had someone there to remind me why I was going to anyway. No one told me I should gain weight, but suddenly I wanted to. I made a conscious decision to take back the fullness of my life, the bountiful body I'd been depriving myself of. In the coming months, I gained something close to 30 pounds. Eventually I stopped weighing myself and destroyed my scale in a fire ceremony in a barbeque pit on my balcony. I felt strong, radiant, and fully alive.

The little girl who had been afraid to be a woman, the sickly child who thought it was her destiny to die, had been transformed into a full-bodied woman simply radiating with joy. When I look back at pictures, I can actually see my skin glowing, as if a raging fire had been lit within me. One day in Kristi's class, out of nowhere I just broke into song:

> *Happy is the heart that still feels pain. Darkness drains and light will come again. Swing open up your chest and let it in. Just let the love, love, love begin.*

Kristi's mouth dropped open, and her eyes welled up with tears. My hand flew to my mouth – I myself couldn't believe that the voice had come out of me. The entire class, which had been silent up until that point, broke into laughter and applause. When people say "I'm so happy I could sing," well . . . I really was.

The darkness that I'd been enrapt in was falling away like the shell of a newly hatched chick. For so long, I'd come to my mat to run away from myself. Now I came to connect. The desire to practice forced me out of my isolation and into meaningful interactions with people. The community I discovered as a result became a source of support and connection beyond anything I ever imagined. I learned to be vulnerable in yoga, to be seen and, ultimately, to be loved by others.

Moving Forward

So here I am, six and a half years later – a writer, researcher, yoga teacher, and community organizer. If you'd told me that day in Whole Foods that I would be teaching yoga in eating disorder centers and traveling the country as a writer, I never would have believed you. I still wake up everyday half-expecting to be in that hospital bed and discover that my life over the past year has all been a fabulous dream. The fact that I'm this happy scares the shit out of me.

My hope is that this story will be helpful to people who are grappling with their own inner demons in silence and isolation. Whether it's an eating disorder, abandonment, depression or addiction, my message to you is this:

> *You don't have to suffer alone. There are people out there who want to love you, who would be honored to bear witness to your pain. Healing doesn't happen in a vacuum. We are human and we have an inherent need to see and be seen, to touch and be touched. No one heals heartbreak alone. Allow yourself to be vulnerable, to be mirrored in the eyes of someone else. Notice what is reflected back, both the beautiful and the grotesque. You are all of it.*

For the broader community, I hope my story will serve to diminish the stigma and misperceptions around eating disorders. I hope it sheds some light on what's happening in the minds of women so skeletal that you flinch when you catch sight of their spine popping out in downward dog. I hope it provokes some questions about how yoga can best be used to serve this population. Many of us have been taught that people with eating disorders simply want to be skinny, that they feel like they have to look like the models on magazine covers to be worth anything, or that they just have an unhealthy "need for control." Those are all symptoms of an eating disorder, not the cause.

I didn't starve myself because I wanted to be skinny. I starved myself because I didn't have the inner resources to cope with the chaos around me. I starved myself because I wanted to reclaim control over my body, because my own mother had rejected me, because I believed myself unworthy of nourishment and love. I starved myself because I'd lost all connection with who I was: my goodness, my worth, the light within we

all bow to when we say, "Namaste." I starved myself because I wanted
to die.

I hated my body *because* I hated myself, not the other way around.
All the downward facing dogs and positive affirmations in the world
weren't going to change that. As much as I wish it could be, yoga isn't
magic. These poses don't cure cancer or mend heartbreak by themselves.
In fact, as I've discussed in this essay, the physical practice can very easily become a tool we use to detach, numb, and even injure ourselves.
The quality of our practice is directly related to the quality of our mind.
Before we start prescribing yoga across the board for people with eating
disorders, addiction issues, and other types of trauma, I think it's worth
taking the time to examine the risks as well as the rewards.

Eating disorders are prevalent in the yoga community, I would argue
even more so than the general population. Many hide their self-destructive behaviors under the guise of detoxing, cleansing, or a pseudo-spiri-
tual path to enlightenment. When I first started teaching, I was forced
to confront shadows of my former self nearly every week. Grossly underweight women would show up for my classes, and quite frankly, I was
afraid to let them practice. The fact is, when an eighty-pound woman
walks into a hot Power Yoga class, she puts herself (and the studio) at
risk of a heart attack. Anorexia is the single most deadly mental illness,
and many women with this disorder die from cardiac-related injuries. I
don't know what the "right thing to do" as a yoga teacher is in that situation. But as a community, I think we should be talking about it.

At the same time, I don't want to suggest that yoga is "too dangerous" for women with eating disorders. I would not be where I am in my
recovery today if I hadn't discovered this practice. As valuable as the
hundreds of hours I spent in therapy were to my long-term development, the psychological approach I was prescribed in treatment was not
enough by itself. For years, I believed if I could just figure out the root
cause of my eating disorder, pinpoint exactly what childhood trauma
had fucked me up so badly, all my urges and negative feelings would

go away. I was taught by well-intentioned mental health professionals that I needed to stop listening to my body, that trusting it would lead me astray. Yes, that model of recovery helped me survive. But it only deepened the fracture between my body and mind; I had to re-connect in order to thrive.

By itself, therapy actually became something of a crutch. It allowed me to ignore the disconnect I felt between my mind and body, philosophize my way around my emotions rather than viscerally experience them. What's more, I became dependent on my therapist for intimacy, allowing a professional relationship to substitute for meaningful connections with others. True healing required I leave the safety of the therapy room – enter the raw, messy world of relationships beyond the proverbial couch. I had to experience myself as someone who was cherished as more than a client or student, but as a human being valued in her own right. When the therapeutic relationship I was in finally came to an end, I was forced to seek support and companionship with the people in my life. It wasn't until that fell away that I really began to trust myself.

Yoga, therapy, nutritional counseling, and residential treatment can be invaluable resources to someone seeking to heal from an eating disorder. But I think it's important to recognize that each are merely tools, resources that should be used with intelligence and thoughtfulness to support the healing process. Therapy should be a safe container that allows us to create the foundation we need to do our real work in the world, not escape from it. Yoga should be a practice we use to strengthen and nurture ourselves, not create further disease. How we use these tools is up to us.

Regardless of whether you've had an eating disorder or not, we all grapple with pain, loneliness, and desperation. One of the greatest lessons I've gleaned from my experience is that healing from anything – especially an eating disorder – requires that we look outside of ourselves as well as within. I am alive today thanks to the kindness of those who have loved me, people who offered a hand of support when my legs weren't strong enough to carry me. Yoga, in my experience, is a practice that brings us into community, connection, and ultimately the greatest healing force of all – Love.

Love is our true destiny. We do not find the meaning of life by ourselves alone – we find it with one another.

— Thomas Merton

Note: I would not be here today without the support of many people not specifically named in this essay, but who nonetheless played a tremendous role in my recovery. Thank you Honey, Lana, Sherry, Betsy, Sophia, Gaynell, Jim, Melody, Holly, Dave, Jen, Alex, Amy, Sarah, Ife, and Michala.

6

Yoga and the 12 Steps:
Holistic Recovery from Addiction

Tommy Rosen

On the night I almost died from smoking crack, there was no conscious understanding of what was happening in my mind or body. I was reduced to a state of depravity, like an animal whose only purpose was to never come down from the rush of this high. I had also smoked a lot of pot that day. Once you start smoking cocaine, however, you no longer feel the effects of pot, so it loses its importance quickly. Not the case with cigarettes, though. Cocaine and cigarettes enjoy each other's company. I had chain-smoked cigarettes for 10 hours that day – but not just any cigarettes. When I did coke, I smoked weird, strong cigarettes – Export A's (The Blue Ones), Camel Straights, occasionally Marlboro Reds and of course, Djarum Clove Cigarettes – anything that packed a punch. If I didn't feel them when they went in, they were too weak.

People who smoke crack together are stoic and precise in their communication. At first, as the initial preparation of coke is being cooked (we used to cook it ourselves into freebase), the participants (never more than three or four) may exchange mischievous smiles or amazingly cynical jokes. But inevitably, the verbal communication becomes less and less until finally the only words uttered are those needed to allow the "partying" to continue. There really are no pleasantries because nothing about this ritual is too pleasant. There is, of course, the walloping initial high produced by taking a big hit while everyone looks on as if they are watching you have an orgasm because in some sick, shadowy way, you are. Then everyone else wants to have the same experience over and over again, even though it lasts such a short time. It is horribly vacuous and in the end leaves you devoid of life force, crying like a man who realizes he has lost everything because for that night, at least, you have lost everything. Eventually, you will lose everything for good.

Breath and (Near) Death

In those days, I was only aware of my breath when I smoked drugs or exercised. Yes, I actually exercised. I loved sports and fancied myself an athlete. How could someone be caught up in a destructive behavior like smoking crack and still have another life that permitted athletics? Well, I grew up with sports and excelled at them. In this particular phase of my life, though, sports took an increasingly distant back seat to drugs. And of course, by the time one starts doing drugs like freebase or heroin, sports and all other efforts are done for. The fact is that one really can't be in both worlds for very long. Kind of like how light and darkness can't co-exist in the same place.

On the night I almost died, I had smoked everything I could get my hands on — tons of cigarettes, marijuana and cocaine. I was lying back on a cushion and started to feel like *I could no longer get a full breath.* Strangely, I was embarrassed and did not want anyone to notice that something was wrong. Possibly, I was dying. But since it was not yet bad enough to pull the ripcord, I played it off for a moment. I closed my eyes and waited. Quickly, the feeling worsened to the point where I could no longer get much of a breath at all.

I stood up and walked out of the room. Panicked and gasping, I thought to myself, "OK, this is it. Game over. Call 911. It all ends tonight. If I survive this and God, I beg of you, that I do, I will go to rehab and get it together." I leaned over and put my hands on my knees like a football player who has had the wind knocked out of him. Very slowly, my body acted on its God-given instinct to survive. My brain sent out the chemicals that my blood stream needed to dilate my bronchial tubes. I began to breathe. The moment of panic passed. Soon that night of horror would end.

Most people probably can't understand why anyone would put himself through such an ordeal time and time again. In the face of so much pain, demoralization, and near death, why would anyone keep using drugs? Such behavior seems to counter everything that we understand about human beings and our innate will to live. But that's the nature of addiction. If given an opportunity to become full-blown, addiction counters even our natural impulse to survive.

I would not end up calling 911. Nor would I go to the hospital. I would not be arrested and go to jail. I did not end up in the insane asylum. I did, however, wake up one day not too long after the night I almost lost my breath for good and realize that I had no next move. I had taken the horror further than I ever had before and spent three nights awake smoking cocaine. I had momentarily duped a drug dealer into fronting me an ounce and had every good intention of selling it to make a tidy profit. Unfortunately, once we got into the coke there was scant chance any of it would be sold. It took a few guys and me three days to smoke our way through it. Finally, racked with pain from being dehydrated, malnourished, exhausted, and hopped up out of my skull, I coerced a friend into giving me several sleeping pills, which finally knocked me out for 30 hours straight. How I survived that, I will never know.

Waking Up

I did not know where I was when I woke up. Looking around my room and house, I saw only squalor. I was beyond terror. I had run out of drugs and alcohol. I had no girlfriend to take care of me. I had no money and no connections left. I owed a drug dealer a lot of money. There was no next move. I was beaten.

I picked up the phone and called my father, the person I relied upon for care and affection when I needed it most. I told him how bad things were, how I had no girlfriend or friends to speak of. How this had happened and that had happened. I told him everything – except for the truth. Then he simply stated, "You're on drugs. I know you're on drugs! Aren't you?" I said, "Yes, Dad, I am."

He said bluntly that I was going to have to go to rehab. I bluntly replied that I would not go. There was a silence on the phone that lasted about 10 seconds. Then I realized my father had started to cry. In his own way, he was as defeated as I was.

That was the straw that broke the camel's back. All of my arrogance and stubbornness fell to the side as I glimpsed the effect that my behavior had on my Dad. The next day, I flew to his home in Los Angeles. He had insisted on seeing me before I went to rehab. I spent four days with him. All in all, we got along pretty well. He was glad to see me alive. We did not speak about much. I slept a lot. After four days, I was off to rehab at Hazelden in Minnesota. My time in hell was coming to an end.

Twelve Steps

It's important to consider the historical context of addiction and the way our society treats it in order to understand how yoga fits into a path of recovery – and how it doesn't.

Let's back for a moment at this history and imagine Bill Wilson, the founder of Alcoholics Anonymous, in the moments just before his spiritual awakening. It's 1935. He finds himself in a hospital room for the umpteenth time, having somehow survived yet another day of alcoholic torture that most folks could not conjure in their worst nightmares. He is utterly beaten down, frightened of everything, and certain that there is no way out of his situation. When he's released from the hospital, despite what he knows, he will drink again as he always has before. With each new episode, he feels that much worse that God has decided to keep him around another day. His wife, friends, and relations feel the frustration of powerlessness, sadness, anger, and betrayal.

From this point in 1935 reaching back in time to the beginning of recorded history, there had been no known solution to the problems of alcoholism and drug addiction. Alcoholics and addicts usually ended up in jails, hospitals, and insane asylums after being ostracized by friend and foe. With little to no success, doctors, religious leaders, psychologists, gurus, and shamans had tried for centuries to deal with these people who just could not stop destroying their lives. To be an active alcoholic at any point in history was a terrible fate. But to have been one before this day in 1935 was to be basically without hope.

Though no one could have known it at the time, that day in 1935 was a turning point for the human race. Like Buddha under the Bodhi Tree, Jesus' Sermon on the Mount, Moses and the Ten Commandments, and Mohammed's Revelations, humankind was about to have a massive divine download. It would pass through the least likely of places, the heart of a life long, raging alcoholic named Bill Wilson.

On that day, Bill was struck "awake" and a magical idea flooded into his thoughts that would positively affect the lives of millions of people who previously had little chance of recovery. The seed ideas, the core of his enlightenment, were these: If I connect with and put my faith in a power greater than myself (read: God) and if I can speak to another alcoholic and share my experience, strength, and hope with them, then I will be able to recover from this hopelessness known as alcoholism. Bill Wilson and a doctor friend of his known as Dr. Bob went on to develop the 12-Step program of Alcoholics Anonymous. Out of this basic framework, a dozen or so other programs have sprung forth over the last 76 years. Today, literally millions of people credit the 12 Steps with saving their lives.

I, too, came to recover from acute drug addiction through the 12 Steps, which I was encouraged to adopt in rehab. The 12 Steps are a spiritual path, incorporating psychology, behavior modification, community participation, and selfless service. The core principle always remains to carry this message to others who still suffer. For 12 years, I worked the program to the best of my ability. There was an enormous amount of reflection, self-study, journaling, working with a sponsor and various therapists, going to meetings, and working with others. A lot of life happened during this time. My relationships with my family and friends improved drastically. I saw success and something less than success in business. I met and married my amazing wife. I also lost both my parents. Day by day, with the support and love of many people, combined with the willingness to try things differently, my life changed in miraculous ways – just as promised.

However, the day would eventually come when my way of thinking and reacting to life, which was still grounded in the energy of addiction, would result in several emotional bottoms and leave me utterly crushed. The 12 Steps had laid a foundation for my recovery. But there was inner work I needed to get to that required something else. This was confusing and difficult, for I had developed a belief that the 12 Steps were all that I needed to navigate everything that life brought my way. I generally felt that I had done the necessary work to live the life that I was being called to live. But something was missing.

I now believe that the 12 Steps took me just far enough down the road to recovery where I was ready and able to pursue deeper work. Despite hearing countless stories detailing how dangerous it is to leave, my path was leading away from 12-Step rooms. I was being pulled toward the deep, powerful well of Kundalini yoga and meditation.

Yoga and the Ego

I first came to yoga in 1991. I walked off the street into Janet Macleod's Iyengar class in San Francisco. I had never seen a person move with so much freedom. I knew that I wanted that right away.

My early relationship with yoga, like my early recovery from drug addiction, was primarily physical and quite uncertain. Intellectually, I understood that both the 12 Steps and yoga were spiritual paths. Beyond that, I made no further connection between the two. I looked at yoga primarily as an athletic endeavor, which brought me a great sweat, increased my strength, and would eventually bring me flexibility.

I put a lot of "ego" into it. I practiced and thought about how my body looked. Or how someone else's body looked. Or how I was attracted to some girl in the room — or to *every* girl in the room. I was obsessive about form and a perfectionist about alignment. I wanted to do it all correctly, but I lacked humility and patience.

And so the great promises of yoga did not come to me except as glimpses of hope interspersed with injuries and frustration. Of course, I got injured. Anyone with the right combination of ego, arrogance, and impatience will have to face himself eventually. For me, it came in the form of back injuries. The typical cycle was to practice hard, overstretch, and not be connected to my breath. I would still feel blissed-out after practice. This afterglow would last until the next day, when my whole body seemed to contract. I'd get super-tight, particularly in the hamstrings, which pulled on my pelvis and lower spine. All that tightness, coupled with the biochemistry of stress and a sugar-rich diet, makes for a bad lower back.

This went on for a while. I was learning to be patient and humble through the school of hard knocks. Eventually, these "unfortunate" physical experiences would ready me for a profound spiritual awakening. I would become so beaten down by my approach to life (even in recovery) that I developed a neurological disease resulting in a painful back condition that left me debilitated for over a year.

Back to the Breath

In 2003, with pain and fear, I hobbled into the office of the man who would become my life teacher. One of the first things he told me was that he knew how I was going to die. Cynically, I responded, "Okay, tell me. How am I going to die?"

"On an exhale," he plainly stated.

My mind quickly ran through a number of death scenarios and I found the statement to be true. We all go on an exhale. He then followed this up with "and of course, you were born on an inhale, like everyone else."

This was Guruprem Singh Khalsa's introduction to the importance of breath in our lives. One's entire life is bookmarked by the first inhale and last exhale. In between these points, our breath is essentially continuous. In the hierarchy of needs in the human body, breath is number one. We can go with out food and even water for a relatively long time, but without precious oxygen carried into our lungs, we are "forced to exit" in a matter of minutes.

Over the next five years, Guruprem met with me regularly in a sort of modern-day apprenticeship. He taught me how to breathe and move with grace through time and space. He taught me how to use my breath to control my mind. And he gave me a vision of a life that existed beyond addiction, even for someone like me who had gone so far down into the darkness.

A heightened awareness of my own breath has linked the major turning points in my life. I hit bottom in my drug addiction in that one, terrifying moment when I feared that I'd lost my ability to pull in the next breath. My teacher shared with me the simple yet profound idea that I — like everyone else on this planet — was born on an inhale. He showed me the way to an even deeper recovery from addiction by emphasizing the elemental importance of breath from the moment I met him. As I dedicated myself to the path of yoga, I came to know the incredible healing potential of working with the breath.

All addiction comes from a sense of lack, a core feeling that something is missing. Ironically, when we breathe poorly, we inadvertently send a signal to every cell in our body that our most core need is not being met. There is a lack. Every part of our being picks up this signal. It creates a pattern of pervasive tension in the mind-body. And because people who struggle with addictions usually breathe poorly, they tend to reinforce this underlying sense of lack with every shallow or rushed breath that they take.

In yoga, we learn to pay closer attention to our breath. We practice techniques that help us deepen and work with it consciously. We clear energy and get present. In so doing, we send new signals to our mind-body, communicating a sense of wholeness. This begins the process of true recovery in that it centers us in our true Self. This is one of the most powerful ways we can stack the odds against relapsing into destructive patterns.

Breath is one of the greatest tools we have. By controlling it, we can access our endocrine system without the use of drugs, alcohol, or other stimuli. Through powerful *Pranayama* exercises, yogis have been leveraging the power of "the infinite pharmacy within" for thousands of years. We have these same capacities today. Realizing that there is something you can do to change your mood, which simultaneously strengthens your body is pretty amazing. Once you experience it and feel the power that comes from mastery of mind, body, and breath, there is no turning back.

I've come to believe that addiction is not possible where there is a conscious awareness of breath. Put another way, the more we are aware of our breath and its importance, the further we move from the dis-ease of addiction – and closer we will be to the ease of living in connection with our true Self. These are powerful, yet simple lessons, which took me a long time to grasp and implement in my life.

Recovery Requires Community

I believe that yoga is this powerful and important. You might, therefore, assume that I think it is all you need for recovery from addiction. On the contrary, I think that dropping a 12-Step program to focus on yoga could be a terrible, and even dangerous decision for a person in recovery to make.

I've never seen a person in acute addiction recover without two things: A spiritual path and a community to support it every single day. The 12-Step program provides both. Yoga — at least as we practice it today — does not.

Yoga is a practice of self-inquiry. It is largely an internal process. We go inside to observe and learn about ourselves. Part of the problem with the application of yoga to addiction is that with addiction, people are already stuck inside themselves. Addiction is a disease of isolation. The first thing we need to do in order to recover is to come into community.

True, we often practice yoga asana in a roomful of other people. But it's astonishingly easy to be isolated in a roomful of yoga practitioners. Typically, you come into class alone. You practice alone. You leave alone. This may be perfectly fine for people who are not in the throws of addiction. If you come to a class with solid connections to your self and others, you may be ready for the deep internal exploration that yoga provides. But addicts have lost their sense of connection to themselves. And unless they're involved in a 12-Step program or an equivalent, they're not part of a community that's going to help them find it again.

Of course, if you were severely addicted, it's highly unlikely that you would find your way into a yoga class and return regularly. But what would happen if you did? Filled with confusion, fear and insecurity, you would enter a roomful of people and begin to breath and move. You would sweat and detox a bit, which is good. But you probably wouldn't have the internal resources necessary to explore yourself in a healing way, much less understand what you are experiencing. As a result, to the extent that you opened up to the deeper dimensions of yoga, it might feel scary or destabilizing. And when the class was over, you would be released back into the world . . . alone. This might leave you even more vulnerable to the immensely powerful cravings of addiction than you were already.

To recover from addiction, you must have a community, a *Sangha*, that understands what you are experiencing and can support you through the massive transformation necessary to recover your connection to all things. The 12-Step program creates such a community and invites you to become part of it. It provides you with a safe container in which you can explore a new way of being in the world. It takes you out of isolation and into connection with others who understand how critical and difficult the path you are walking is because they are doing the same thing themselves.

Integrating Mind, Body, and Spirit

Ultimately, the energy of addiction is rooted in a disconnection from our own spirit, that mysterious core of our being that carries consciousness and permits life itself. At the same time, addiction distorts us mentally, physically, and spiritually. That's why it's so difficult to "cure."

Both the 12 Steps and the path of yoga address the spiritual aspect of this dis-ease. They do so, however, in very different ways. In particular, they harness different physical and mental energies, different capacities of our bodies and minds.

By providing a "blueprint for living" and connecting us to a supportive community, the 12 Steps provides the foundation we need to reconnect to ourselves. We meet with other recovering addicts. We share a common space. We feel each other's presence. We listen to each other's stories. We bear witness to each other's struggles. In so doing, we physically root ourselves in the nurturing soil of a supportive community.

There's also an important mental dimension to this process. Addiction clouds our thinking and judgment. The 12 Steps provide a pathway to a deep mental detoxification. Through this framework, we come to understand the nature of addiction. It gives us a common anguage to articulate that knowledge, and creates a forum that allows us to think through where we've been and where we want to go in conversation with others.

Most importantly, the 12 Steps connects us to the spirit of the Universe, which people in the program refer to as "a power greater than ourselves." Ultimately, it is this spiritual connection that heals and empowers us.

The work of yoga is quite different, though the end goal is the same. Rather than directing our attention outward to connect with others, we bring it inward to connect internally. This process of connection is subtle. It works in a realm without words.

Through the body, breath, and mental focus we walk the inner landscape and clear the path toward connection and liberation.

While yoga engages our minds, it works primarily with our intuitive, subconscious, and extra-rational capacities. This is quite different from the rational understandings and verbal communications facilitated by a 12-Step community. Similarly, yoga works with the body in a unique way. Rather than showing up to be physically present with others, we dive into the mystery of our own embodiment.

Regulating the breath, focusing the mind, and working the body through yoga asana progressively clears the energy channels of the body/mind. We slowly undo the damage of addiction on a cellular level. As we "get the issues out of our tissues," we free ourselves from the chains of the past. And breath is the key that unlocks this process, providing the crucial connection between body and mind.

Through this synergy of mind, body, and breath, yoga connects us to the same sense of being a part of "something greater than ourselves" that we arrive at through the 12 Steps. The path that leads there, however, runs through different capacities of the body/mind. Working these additional aspects of ourselves, I believe, constitutes a necessary part of "advanced recovery." While it complements and deepens the 12 Steps, it is fundamentally different from them as well.

Holistic Recovery

Since addiction takes a holistic approach to destroying a human being's life, recovery must take a holistic approach to putting that life back together. We know that to break an acute addiction takes an incredible amount of power. It requires more than just putting down drugs and alcohol. It requires a combination of ingredients that together, provide what is necessary to move beyond addiction.

The 12 Steps are the most successful method we have to enable recovery from addictions of all kinds. Working them for 12 years broke the addictions that had sent me into hell and almost killed me. The 12 Steps educated me about the nature of my problem and connected me to a community of people that supported me on my path to recovery. It reconnected me with my own spirituality. This enabled me to live a life worth living.

Eventually, however, I found that the 12 Steps alone were not enough. I needed to cleanse away the detritus that addiction had left in the cells of my body and hidden chambers of my mind. I needed to learn how to harness the power of my own breath for healing. I found what I needed in yoga. I needed something capable of bringing me into even deeper into connection with my true Self.

Since that night when I almost let drugs take my last breath, yoga and the 12 Steps have provided me with the necessary tools to have a truly holistic recovery: a supportive community, knowledge of addiction, ability to work with breath, tools for mind/body cleansing and integration, and a connection with my true Self and the infinite Universe. Today, I'm grateful to be able to share what I've learned with others.

Looking back to the time when I was smoking crack, I never could have imagined that one day I'd be teaching Yoga for Addiction Recovery with a sense of purpose, passion, and fulfillment. I feel infinitely fortunate to have learned about yoga and the 12 Steps, a holistic one-two punch to overcome addiction.

There's an epidemic of addiction in our society today — ranging from the "big five" of drugs, food, money, sex, and alcohol to more intangible issues such as chronic fear, resentment, and self-doubt — and we need such powerful mind-body-spirit medicine to not only recover and heal, but actively grow and prosper. It's a blessing to have found this practice, and an honor to teach it to others.

7

Modern Yoga Will Not Form a Real Culture Until Every Studio Can Also Double As a Soup Kitchen, and other observations from the threshold between yoga and activism

Matthew Remski

I have self-identified as a yoga practitioner for ten years now. Through practices and practice periods ranging from mild to intense, I've gained considerable self-awareness, emotional constancy, personal integrity. I have rediscovered my body, and learned how to commit to the present moment, almost at will. These gifts have radiated into my writing, helped me to parent, taught me to listen to my clients, helped me serve a friend who was mentally ill, helped me survive the death of a close friend, and are currently a life-raft through a difficult divorce.

But I am lonely, because my chosen path is not contained or supported by a coherent culture. It has no family infrastructure. It offers no life-transition rituals. It does not marry or bury us. It does not host AA meetings. It runs no soup kitchens. I don't need yoga to be a religion. I need it to provide community. Community that acts consciously and pragmatically for the common good. Community that is not bankrupted by its exclusive consumer classism. Community that reaches out as much as it reaches in.

my catholic relapse

My journey with this theme begins with how I became catholic again, for about two hours.

It was a few springtimes ago: tender buds under a tender sun. I was nostalgic for youth and family, and especially singing. I biked to Thomas Aquinas Chapel at the University of Toronto with dew on my fenders. I had taken first communion there, 33 years gone by. I didn't know I was about to take second communion that morning.

The choir members are in their early 20s. Babies sing along. Little girls shine like pennies in their Sunday dresses. Boys pull on sleeves and ask where the priest lives. The yellowed hymnbook smells like 1922. I run my hand along a groove in the pew and the wax of an earlier time curls up under my fingernail while the sun pours through rippling leaded glass. An ecstasy grows, of childhood memory, of the softest kind, pictures and sensations that echo in a primal womb. I don't find this space anywhere else. A quiet rapture in the warmth of worn stone and the ambient swell of a collective breath. I open, finally, once again, to the openness of children, who watch, and listen, and let the spectacle of life flow in.

As churches go, it is a good church – social action, thinking people, cultural diversity, folks with *projects*, an old Victorian rectory that feels like a union hall, a grand piano beside the altar, Jesuits who read Tagore. A well-cooked masala of catholic communalism, frankincense, paraffin soot, and nasty perc coffee only drinkable with lots of sugar and cream.

It had me. The damn church had me so melted that I could forgive the psychotic Old Testament reading and the clumsy homily apologizing for it. I shook hands with an ancient man to the left of me, and played with the toy truck of the four-year-old boy to the right. I took communion (first wafer in 25 years?), shivering at Jesus' line: *This is my body*. Yes: this is my body: this bread, these people, this human condition. I couldn't sing at communion because yearning was a star in my throat.

But what happened after communion sealed the deal. A woman took the podium to give housekeeping announcements for the parish. Mondays: a mentorship program. Tuesdays: blanket drive for the homeless. Wednesdays: AA meeting. Thursdays: bereavement support group. Friday: teen dance. Saturday: Tiny Shrouds Society.

I turned to the old man. "Tiny Shrouds?"

He had watery eyes. Underweight, and a quiver in his right hand. He whispered "A few of the gals get together and knit little shrouds for the babies that die every week in the hospitals."

That did it: I lost it. Was this the church I'd left so many years ago in a storm of disillusionment and cynicism? A place with such kindness, such organized empathy? What had I replaced it with? A solitary, countercultural path. I'd developed my breath, my internal observer, powers of inquiry. But now I should probably get in line for the Tuesday blanket. Had yoga made me homeless? Where were the studio food drives? Who was knitting the shrouds? Where was the yoga studio that sat in the middle of this dirty and vibrant life and facilitated its suffering and hopeful economy?

Surely this is harsh. Yoga is a cultural adolescent in our age, driving forward on the fumes of counterculture disillusionment, wanting more than the known patterns, wanting more than what we're programmed to expect. It wants self-expression and constant redefinition. Young and dumb and full of possibility, yoga is also looking in the mirror, wondering how it looks. Today, yoga is more about identity than it is about service. Yoga's just getting started here — we wish it well. We really do.

You can't ask a teenager to suddenly manifest a social service network that the churches have been mothering for generations. The churches have paid their mortgages through centuries of focused intention and tithing. (And feudalism, and colonial economy, and collusion with the state . . . but don't get me started.) Can we really expect yogis to run soup kitchens while we're still making our rent? And as long as there are churches that corner the market in binding people in this love that transcends dogma because it *acts*, studios will offer a much thinner product: classes, self-help tools, self-discovery adventures to tropical paradises. It may be another generation before the patina of real community starts to glow.

I wonder. Will our yoga studios ever run with children and the tears of alcoholics? Will we tithe ourselves? Will we take all of this self-work and turn it inside out, and show our societies that we have as much food as wisdom, as much politics as peace, as much home as *Om*?

Will we take over these well-worn buildings when the last of the clerics fall into disgrace or simple irrelevance? When the last and bitterest shreds of moral hypocrisy and intellectual bankruptcy rupture the last congregations, will we rejuvenate their networks with a kinder vision of human relationship and ecology? Will we buy up dilapidated churches for pennies during the next crash and put them in collective yogic trust? If we did, could we shake up yoga's stunting, competitive, commercial model through which we've been propagating our spirituality? Will we be up to the task?

two deaths in two cultures

Another story. My friend, a South Indian accountant/Sanskrit scholar/ sitar master/polymath, told me how he'd encountered two very different examples of yoga community dealing with tragedy.

On the same day, two men that he knew died in car accidents: both married, both with children, both in their 40s. One was a parishioner at the Hindu temple where my friend serves as a Vedic priest. The other was the husband of a yoga practitioner at one of the western-type yoga studios where my friend moonlights as a Sanskrit lecturer for teacher trainings.

Within twelve hours of the Hindu man's death, a meeting was called at the temple. Several hundred parishioners showed up to organize care for the widow and children. Someone pledged six months of cooking. Another pledged house maintenance for a year. A group of women offered childcare. The widow's boss agreed to an extended leave of bereavement, with full salary and benefits. This was all accomplished before the formal memorial plans even began to take shape.

Five days after the temple meeting, my friend received an e-mail newsletter from the studio where the other new widow had been practicing. It was generated by template through Constant Contact. The image was a lotus, and the text was typical condolence-copy: "Studio X is very sad to announce the passing of Y. May we keep his family in our hearts." The newsletter advertised no meeting to organize family service, didn't direct anyone to a charity fund for the survivors, and didn't list funeral details. My friend ached for the man's family, and the studio community, which did not seem to have any protocol for mourning, nor was gathering material support an obvious first step. My friend said: "I was not asked to do anything."

I want to figure out how we can ask ourselves as yoga practitioners and teachers to do more.

caveats for those who read further

This article critiques the resistance of "modern western yoga culture" (MWYC) to social coherence and activism. So I really should define MWYC as I'm using it for the purposes of this analysis. I'm speaking to the present, majority audience and milieu of this book: yoga practitioners who are North American or Western European, based in studios that focus primarily on asana instruction. This is the emergent culture that I wish to call out and provoke. I'm not referring to modern Indian yoga, with its televised saints and extensive ashram infrastructure that nurtures India's long-standing religious heritage of charitable ethics.

There is a second usage of the word "modern" in this article that has nothing to do with late capitalism or stretch pants (at least on the surface). This usage denotes the psychohistorical epiphany of "modern consciousness," as described by Julian Jaynes and others. Modern consciousness emerges in the envelope surrounding the Axial Age (800 BCE to 200 CE, cf. Karl Jaspers), which features a revolutionary transition to individualism and an implosion of interior abstract space that eventually spawns the private self (an innovation measured by the appearance of personal agency in world literature at about the time of the *Odyssey*). The private self is a crucial character for our study. For it is the private self that both seeks enlightenment and can dissociate from its ecology in the ecstasy of personal concern. It is the modern and private self that Siddhartha chased into the forest of his inquiry. It is the modern and private self that is the customer of the MWYC studio. (And the customer is always right.) But the public self, the social self, the political self, the ecologically dependent self, the empathetic self: these selves are as yet underserved by our yoga.

Lastly: something I've learned from presenting this polemic publicly over the past year. I have needlessly hurt a lot of feelings by failing to make one thing clear: If you are reading this article and interested in this material, you are probably already in the yoga-social-activism choir, and my critique is most likely not applicable to your own innovative and exploratory practice. I have no illusions about changing the minds of any readership. My purpose is to simply describe the tensions that I think we all feel in our unconscious yearning for active community. May new paths illuminate themselves from this description.

yoga's antisocial heritage

For many of us, the first experience of yoga is revelatory. Amidst the steel and glass of our banality and dissociation, asana and breath reconnect us with *lebensweld*, to use Husserl's term: the undulating dialogue of self and world, now so often obscured by technology, abstraction, McFood and public McSpace. Our first class feels personal, intimate, and embodied. Many of us exit space and time entirely during that first *savasana*. These experiences uniquely prepare us for empathy. Somewhere we realize: *everyone has access to this spaciousness, this relaxation, this non-reactivity*. But it is an empathy we haven't the means to share if we're not behaving like a culture. Ten minutes of camaraderie in the changeroom after a sweaty class will not organize a soup kitchen.

There are real structural challenges to yoga community: the commercial model, the transient population of students, the collusion of vacation and retreat, practice sequences as commercial products, and asana as a therapeutic that plateaus in its effectiveness at the three-year mark for most practitioners. I'll discuss these later. I'll start at the source: psychosomatic obstacles to the formation of yoga community that run as deep as the tradition itself.

"Let him wear a single garment," declares the *Vashista Sutra*, "or cover his body with a skin or with grass that has been nibbled by a cow. Let him sleep on the bare ground. Let him frequently change his residence, dwelling at the threshold of the village, in an empty house, or at the root of a tree. Let him constantly seek the knowledge of his heart. Let him belong to no tribe nor follow any dogma. Let him, though not mad, appear like one out of his mind."

Throughout the vast majority of its 2,500-year history, much of yoga has been a deeply anti-social practice. Through its many threads, it has resisted the values of householding, genteel mores, the rules of caste, and the "bondage" of human attachments. Yoga has arisen whenever social patterns need to be broken, whenever cosmological concepts reach turgid banality, whenever new *being* is ready to destroy old *thinking*. It has always stood against the status quo. It is a deconstructive art. It has never taken responsibility for the nurturance of social relationship. And except for the nomadic bands of armed Tantric yogis who roamed the countryside of the Raj with knives and guns, attacking, killing and even eating Englishmen wherever they could, yoga has rarely been employed to protect the earth itself from exploitation or imbalance. Yet today, this is precisely what we need yoga for: to restore social and ecological relationship in a time of deepening crises.

yoga as a trauma-response to bicameral breakdown

Whence the anti-social bias within yoga? I believe it comes from the fact that yoga has often arisen as a trauma-response to amplifications of psychosocial tensions. On the micro-level and in my own time, I have seen hundreds of practitioners, including myself, retreat into the interior space of yoga as they digest changed relationships, changed careers, economic displacement, illnesses, and deaths. On the macro-level of anthropology, reaching back into the axial age, yoga performs a similar function, providing a powerful means of negotiating the shift between pre-modern and modern consciousness: a kind of coping mechanism for the dis-ease of an unfamiliar identity. As the present slings and arrows of our personal lives compel self-study and self-learning, the general crisis of modernity opened a vast and uncharted internal space, filled with multiple voices and perspectives. Yoga attempts to make us feel safe within both processes.

Julian Jaynes describes the macro-transition in heart-rending detail in *The Origin of Consciousness in the Breakdown of the Bicameral Mind*. His elegant story deserves a brief overview, which I'll attempt here.

Prior to agriculture, the immediacy of human ecology left little space for feelings of personal agency. Humans felt themselves in direct communication with their world. So possessed by ecological forces (wind, rain, animal, forest sprite) was bicameral man (as Jaynes names him, describing pre-modern thoughts as aural hallucinations zinging from left to right hemispheres) that he had little sense of *personal* decision-making or self-assertion. Achilles does not *decide* to kill his foes: the wind in his lungs moves his arm to lift his spear. Abraham does not *decide* to kill Isaac: a voice from wind and fire commands him so. Nor does self-reflection stay Abraham's knife: it takes another exogenous force – an angel – to save the boy's skin. Bicameral man moved from campsite to campsite because of the game, not because the *signs* of game gave him the *idea* that it might be good to move camp. Bicameral man did not *read* nature. He *was* nature.

This visceral, dreamlike, and claustrophobic oneness between world and flesh was slowly pried apart by tool invention, and stuttering rises in health and longevity and therefore population density, which forced neighboring tribes into closer contact and commerce. Trade necessitated the accommodation of differing points of view, if constant war was to be avoided. Higher mental faculties and political capacities emerge out of these first experiences of intersubjectivity. As inter-tribal trade increased, we began to translate language and concepts, to use symbols, currencies, and other abstractions of value. Our survival became dependent not on being hardwired to the environment, but upon the manipulation of multiple perspectives, protocols, diplomacies, languages, and goals. Human consciousness leapt from nest into network. This change was then compounded by the contemplative leisure time afforded by agriculture, codified with the rise of textuality, and corporatized by the emergence of legal and religious institutions.

In just a few thousand years, humanity goes from the sensual coherence of an immediate animalistic relationship with its ecology to the fray of multiple internal personae negotiating a symbolic world. Now, when you go to the market, you leave your gods and forests behind, because ecology is no longer your governing or protective language. Your local gods cannot be shared with the other, who has his own. You must now be many things for many people and situations. Now, the "truth" is not so obvious, and certainly not to be found in the realm of social exchange and spectacle.

New burning questions arise: out of these many roles, amongst many tribes, and as the roads begin to emerge that will string together great cities of otherness like pearls on a string, we ask: *Who am I? What is true?* No pre-modern human being asks these questions, because there is literally no separate internal agency to ask them. But once that inner person arises and, like a three-year-old, begins to ask the unanswerable, yoga must be born: a quest to commune, to rejoin, to feel grounded in a simpler time. And where are the answers? They can no longer be outside us, for everything outside us changes and is subject to interpretation. Yoga seeks an inner home, an inner identity, and an inner truth. To find these, yoga has often retreated from our original home: the world.

Hence the anti-ecological bias of modern yoga (and perhaps the eco-laziness of MWYC). The very purpose of Patanjali's philosophy is to *amplify* human dissociation from the changeable, dissatisfying environment of eco-social complexity. His sutras appropriate the older sankhyan dualism between *purusha* (consciousness) and *prakriti* (nature), to draw out an escape plan (an *astanga* of cumulative internalization practices) for the human being to isolate himself from his ecology and into a state of catatonic bliss (*kaivalya*). The *sutras* deny evolution (by accepting the *sankhya* creation narrative that consciousness precedes matter), presume class equality amongst practitioners (that everyone is starting in the same place, with the same leisure time), and fail to even once allude to the chaotic reality of love. The Patanjalian legacy, if we actually take it seriously, is completely incoherent with what the majority of MWYC practitioners value. It is a retreating, escapist, transcendental, sense-suppressing, evolution-denying, sexless, childless, artless path that leads to a cave of lonely bliss, from which the mess of the world is blessedly hidden. Patanjali is not at all interested in relationship. But we totally are, and we must be.

Not that we consumers of MWYC are big readers of Patanjali. The *sutras* are more of a branding meme than an influential philosophy in the present day. Regardless, the yoga philosophy we do know and study in the present day does not encourage us to go out and use our newfound peace and balance to organize soup kitchens. Most yoga philosophy, even down to the effusive and often shallow neo-Tantra of our present day (Anusara is a good example) takes the Patanjalian high road, seeking to console the practitioner within a bubble of self-generated peace.

So far for me, yoga has given just the right amount of peace. My level of yoga-peace is like a Winnicottian mother: it's good enough. I'm suspicious of too much peace, in fact — it's a sure sign that I am splitting in some way, and avoiding some shard of rage. These days I need my peace dressed with just the right amount of piss and vinegar to get things done in the world, and to fall hopelessly in love with the Other. Because it is no longer appropriate to our survival to speak of happiness in individualistic and internal terms. We can no longer retreat into ourselves to find happiness. We must meet the Other where she is.

the legacy of the yogic response to modern consciousness

Seeking for the internal and invisible *atman* or soul is what yogis did when they were overwhelmed (perhaps equally fascinated and traumatized) by the absurd complexities of early modern life. Contemplators sought a new internal constancy to weather their social changes, to lift them out of the chaos of nature, and invest their now-solitary hopes in something incorruptible: *personal certainty* and *individual salvation*. I think that when we take a good look at how this arc dovetails with the contemporary promises of consumerism, we'll get closer to understanding why the formation of yoga community is not coming to us naturally.

The yogi of modern consciousness is alone, having retreated from contact with the living world and social realities, and, in malnourished pursuit of the changeless and the spotless, now mourns the natural world with an austere melancholy. Says Patanjali: "All life is suffering for a man of discrimination, because of the sufferings inherent in change and its corrupting subliminal impressions, and because of the way the qualities of material nature turn against themselves." And listen to Jesus: "My god, my god: why have you forsaken me?"

Perhaps my radar for all things doleful and transcendent is a little too sharp, but I feel this same world-evading depression lurking within the zeitgeist of MWYC. I believe that we carry the sentiments of a very early and improvised therapy that may not be serving us anymore. Yoga language seems to carry the dour echo of a traumatic rupture between feeling harmonized and feeling internally lost. Go to YouTube and listen to the old tapes of Sivananda droning on about eternal consciousness. He sounds like Vincent Price: arched, eerie and foreboding. The language of transcendental escape and lyrical mourning abounds. And then there are the obvious signs of disconnection: practitioners coming to me injured from their aggressive Mysore practices, asking for physiotherapy so that they get back to punishing their bodies. They are afraid to tell their Jois-ordained teachers that they are in pain. I tell them to go to restorative class for six months. I rarely see them again.

To the extent that MWYC carries this now-ancient trace of dissociative trauma, it will not be predisposed to the collective concerns of social or ecological justice. Navel-gazing and penitential melancholy do not run soup kitchens. I believe that we have learned enough from the radical subjectivity that yoga has to offer. We now yearn to move towards intersubjectivity. In intersubjectivity, our lives are not ours alone, our experience and resources are utterly shared, and social, political, and ecological conditions are our root concerns, because we recognize that our world makes us. We recognize that the other, from whom Patanjali suggests we flee, makes us.

Of course, our fall into the rabbit-hole of human interiority continues with every scroll and click. Nothing seems to slow it down: we must aggressively re-balance it with re-embodiment and community. I believe that yoga can continue to help us in the navigation of interiority, not as a Patanjalian end-destination, but as a resource towards social coherence. Interiority can definitely give an internal constancy that nurtures *prana*, and a non-reactivity that conserves *prana*. These should not be ultimate goals, but means that equip us to heal our social, political, and ecological crises without being traumatized in the process.

Clinical psychologists at the University of Toronto are currently proposing that "Ecological Stress Disorder" be added to the DSM-IV, to describe the anxious burnout of climate-change activists. Such a person could definitely use yoga – but not to retreat from their passion. Rather: movement and breath that resolved in a contemplative feeling of self-sufficiency might be just the experience that renews their compassion and warriorship.

Without vigorously scrubbing MWYC of its vestigial asceticism, I think we'll continue to feel difficulty in connecting our mat or cushion experience with the rest of life. We'll be distracted by the wish to "perfect" consciousness, rather than driving towards re-integration with the living world and each other. We'll continue to tolerate the ecstatic nihilism of New Age psycho-Ponzi schemes such as *The Secret* in our Facebook news feeds. And socially, there will still be relatively little organized charitable work generated amongst so many empathetic and skilled participants. There will still be inadequate support for the family lives of practitioners. And most embarrassingly, yoga will continue to market itself as a consumer-class consolation, offering a fashionable inner peace to a preciously small fraction of humanity. And in our studios, every beeswax tea-light will cast the shadows of unaddressed alienation and despair.

a studio-to-soup-kitchen transition

A client phoned me from Montreal, wishing to consult on fall schedule changes for her yoga studio. I told her that from the perspective of Ayurveda, restorative yoga should be the staple physical mode, to calm

and warm *vata dosha*. She was intrigued, so I gathered some more data
to flesh out a plan. Her demographic is young and underemployed: grad
students, artists in entry-level positions at design firms. Many folks
getting off work at 5:30 or so. Mostly single, mostly childless, and, like
most denizens of Mile End, they have come from elsewhere, and live in
Montreal studio specials: tiny creaky code-violating apartments with
exposed bulbs and vanishingly small kitchens. It sounded to me like
fertile ground for a yoga-and-community-building experiment.

I proposed a drop-in restorative class for every evening, but with a flex-
ible entrance time. Students could show up anywhere between 5:30 and
6:30, with the understanding that they enter silently. Mats and props and
blankets are preset for students as they come in from the cold: they can
simply enter the flow with whatever posture is happening when they arrive. The room is warm and candlelit. And then from 6:30 to 7pm: gentle
Vinyasa, to spread the restorative *sattva* out into waking life, and the limbs.

Of course the room is also pervaded by the aroma of stew. Because at
about noon that day, an energy exchange student fired up a rice steamer
and a slow cooker in the studio kitchen. (Every studio needs a kitchen if
it will double as a soup kitchen.) The slow cooker bubbles with a rich dal
(split yellow mung with ghee and curry, let's say.) So after *savasana*, the
whole gang peels themselves off the floor, and, still bundled in their blankets, waddle towards the kitchen for a bowl of goodness. Conversation,
networking, and relationship naturally follow. And who wouldn't pay
five bucks extra for a warm meal with friends on the way home to a cold
and lonely apartment? The cost of the bowl of food itself is probably fifty
cents. Coziness doesn't cost money. It simply takes intention, and an eye
on the bigger picture. Inner peace is nice, but what all goes into it?

owning our challenges: infrastructure and the 90% drift

We don't instinctively think this way — yet. It's not surprising. We're
not churches with the benefit of centuries of social infrastructure. We

don't see ourselves as serving a culture, but rather as serving people who seek individual releases and resolutions. MWYC exists as a consumer product, purveyed in commercial spaces with high overheads that necessitate competition between studios, lineages, and teachers. Restorative Soup Kitchen is not a high-profit product. But it may well be a very sustainable product, because it speaks to a broad palette of needs, and begins to shift consumer expectation into communal *noblesse*.

Another key structural obstacle to yoga community is the general arc of self-therapy. For the most part, people come to yoga in the midst of their efforts to resolve a particular issue: an injury, a chronic illness, a period of intensified anxiety or depression, or a transition involving divorce or grieving. Asana feels wonderful, full breathing does wonders, the person experiences improvement, and then the improvement plateaus. They begin to practice at home a little bit, and then a little bit more. Eventually, their yoga learning-curve stops: they know enough about what they need, and perhaps want to try bellydancing or *capoeiria* with their extra free hours that week.

In one way, this is as it should be: yoga studios providing self-care tools that a person can sustainably fold into their general resources for balance and integrity. But in another way, this revolving door shortsells the real potential of the yoga studio to rise into its role as community center. I'm a studio owner who knows dozens of other studio owners, and the consensus is clear: we retain only 10 percent of our students for more than two years, mainly because they commit to a teacher training stream. The other 90 percent comes for the tenure of their issue, and then departs. The turnover requires constant educational and discount marketing, which doesn't leave a lot of time for owners to engage in community building.

But would that 90 percent drift away if the studio offered more? Not "more" in terms of classes, but "more" in terms of cultural services? 90 percent of Catholics do not drift within two years: the tiny shrouds reel 'em back in. I'm willing to bet that student retention skyrockets for the studio that starts to offer "Yoga School" from 3:30-5:30 everyday for 4-6-year-olds, as a yoga-based after-school care program.

what we can do

I'd like to see us stop *talking* about community, and start actually *doing* community.

First: I'd like to see a sign on the door entering every yoga studio that says:

> *you're going inside*
> *to find breath*
> *inner constancy*
> *a memory of all you share*
> *with the world*
> *and each other*

Then, on the way out of the studio, a sign that says:

> *now the world needs*
> *what you have found within.*

Next, I have some proposals for practitioners and studio owners.

for practitioners

1. Study yourself. At what point will your self-therapy be "good enough"? Has it gone beyond this point to become neurotic and self-obsessed? What can you do for others when your self-discoveries plateau?
2. Measure your spiritual evolution by your general capacity for social participation.
3. Work towards an equal balance of self- and other-care. If you go to one-hour asana class, donate another hour to the society.

(Unless of course you're in human services or are parenting young children on a middle-class income or less, in which case your yoga really should be just about you because you're already doing enough for crying out loud . . .)

for studio owners

1. Establish, declare, and publicize a tithe on revenues: this might require overhead reduction, which over time may provoke you to move towards home-based instruction. You have to stop paying rent. More on this in a bit.
2. Pool tithes across multiple studios, for greater investment impact in local projects.
3. Sliding-scale fees to accommodate the un- or under-employed.
4. Make a list of essential government resources that allow your business to thrive. Here in Toronto, a regressive mayoralty is trying to cut public transit to balance a manufactured budget deficit. Every yoga studio in Toronto depends on public transit to bring its students to class. I am the only studio owner I know who has taken any political action on the issue. This is crazy. If the streetcars stop rolling, students stop coming. I say to my fellow owners: *act*. Educate your membership on one issue per month. Depute at City Hall for the programming you rely on. Invite your councilor to speak in your studio.
5. Beyond tithing, establish a committed ratio of income classes to charitable classes.
6. Each studio is in a ward/district/riding: offer space to citizen meetings and town halls. Take advantage of the multi-purpose *sattva* of studio space: anything can happen in it, and probably better.

7. Every studio should have a kitchen. There's nothing more so-cially binding than food. Kitchens are very handy as well when one wishes to run, say, a soup kitchen.

8. Canvas the garden space owned by your student body. Work to-wards facilitating a studio CSA.

9. Family programming, family programming, family programming.

10. Figure out how to greet each new child formally into the circle of your community.

11. Instead of yoga vacays, start offering local vision quests or gue-rilla social service projects.

12. Figure out how to hold affirmation ceremonies for relationships (previously known as weddings).

13. Figure out how to formally support practitioners transitioning through separation or bereavement.

14. Do not pretend that your studio is a suffering-free space. Make it a little rough, a little ragged. Allow it to reflect people's lives. The patina of difficulty will retain more people for better reasons than all of your specialty finishes combined. Yoga is wabi-sabi.

money

There are at least five major yoga studios in Toronto that are paying more than 10K per month in rent. Let's think about this for a minute. It takes 500 student visits per month with each paying $20 per class to cover the rent alone. Add in pass discounts and energy exchange, and then 700 visits are required, perhaps more. Seven hundred visits pulled from a transient demographic that will be brand-loyal for a maximum of two years. Which means you have to add 25 percent marketing to your rent outlay to make sure you never suffer a lull in new attendance. This is all before teachers, admin, web mastering and infrastructure see a penny. In one studio I know, the teachers (like writers) are actually paid last: two dollars per mat up to eight mats, then three dollars per mat for every mat over eight. Teachers at this studio are often trekking across town on the threatened public transit that the owners seem to ignore and slogging back home with twelve bucks in their pocket. But the owners feel stuck because they are dealing with impossible overhead. One of the owners in the 10K/month club runs the most sexily visible studio in town. And every summer when student visits dip, she tells me she has to make a hard decision whether or not to pack it in. Why? Because of unconscionably bad financial sense that provides for no savings and no equity.

Many of the 10K/month club studios have been open for close to a decade, and they have zero equity to show for it. Thousands of classes, tens of thousands of students, countless revelations, *kriyas*, and enjoyments, and millions of dollars: all vanished into the maw of the rent economy, which perpetually threatens with exorbitant hikes. The physical history and ballast of an entire generation of practitioners can be erased by a 5 percent uptick in the rental market when the lease comes due.

If you told the average catholic that of the $20 that he put on the collection plate every Sunday, $1 goes to the office admin, $1 tunes the organ and buys music and hymnbooks, $1 goes to cleaning and altar supplies, $1 goes to the accountant, $1 goes to the missions, $2 goes to maintaining the priest's room and board, and the remaining $13 goes to a landlord who doesn't care one bit about the entire catholic project, he would be disgusted. But this is exactly the economy that we in MWYC are financing. In terms of capital assets, the millions of dollars we spend on ourselves vanish on our collective outbreath. Studios that have served tens of thousands of people can vanish overnight, without the faintest *tadasana* footprint. This doesn't happen with churches, or with temples. It doesn't happen where a group of people have committed to something together, and have given it a place and a name.

Perhaps the most enraging thing of all to me is that many owners in such situations try to make a virtue of their financial ineptitude. "Well, I was never interested in running a studio like this anyway — I just fell into it." Or, "I've always been too interested in my *sadhana* to pay much attention to the banking stuff." Thus the old asceticism comes around in a strange circle: where once it encouraged solipsistic retreat from house-holding, it now provides a template for dissociative business attitudes that serve the few. And for no good reason: yoga business owners not being good enough at business to build equity in and for their communities is now just an anti-social cop-out, plain and simple.

MWYC must stop paying rent, not just to physical landlords, but also to the gods of the market, which ends up being our de facto programming director. When major studios struggle with non-equity-building-overhead year after year, there is continual pressure to sell the big-ticket items: yoga vacations and teacher trainings. I would argue that the former are ecologically unethical, while everyone agrees that the latter are glutting the yoga labor market with marginally trained teachers. But on the day-to-day level, this egregious overhead that vanishes in a cloud of incense demands that each class be popular, i.e., high-yield. And we all know what "popular" means, whether in music, fiction, or yoga workshops. "Yoga and Raw Chocolate" is going to beat out "Using Ayurveda to Support Yoga Practice." And maybe this is as it should be – how can I judge? But it would be nice if we could be sure that capitalism was not the primary arbiter of what directions MWYC takes in its journey of inquiry.

Bottom line: establishing capital assets is essential for community building. We have the politics and temperament that could be gravitating towards co-operative ownership. And, I believe, we have the dollars as well. There are an awful lot of wealthy yoga practitioners out there who would prefer giving money to their yoga parish than to their over-funded *alma mater* every year.

A co-op yoga studio/healing center would be a magnet for community care. It wouldn't be hard to do. Take those 700 visits per month: they represent perhaps 300 students. Of those 300, would 10 percent have the resources and interest to stake 10K into a co-op building purchase? Yes? That's a 300K down payment, 20 percent of a 1.5M property: perhaps enough space for two studios and a kitchen to make soup in. Numbers, numbers: who knows? What is clear is that we have to realize that we are all stakeholders, not only in practices and philosophies, but in the bricks and mortar that shelter our growing hearts.

Want peace that lasts? Pick up a hammer and claim ownership. There's a co-op bike shop in Toronto called Bike Pirates, where you can go and learn to fix your own bike. There's a sign in their window: "Everyone wants a better world, but no one wants to fix their fucking bike chain."

yoga, activism, and identity

My catholic relapse morning brought up so much more for me than the disparity between how yoga and catholic cultures are able to serve baseline human needs. It made me look at the mystery of who I think I am, and how free I feel to meld my various worlds.

I'm sure I can't be catholic for more than a day every few years: this rare emotional regression could never withstand my ethical and metaphysical outrage at catholic bankruptcy. The church is still the church: an authoritarian and uncommunicative bureaucracy of conservatism and fear that runs on sexual violence and stolen land, resists progressive change at every turn, dressed up in a theology as emotionally punitive as it is intellectually absurd. What a paradoxical life this is: I fell in love that morning with the milk of human kindness, which somehow continues to flow out of an abattoir. Clearly, I am called to bring what I value from this gloriously broken thing into my studio, into my practice.

The morning was moving and strange, and left me disarmed. After a little inquiry, I can see that my feelings were splintered, amplified and scrambled by my own internal conflicts about identity and allegiance, and the scars of conversion. Do I still belong to this group? When I rejected it, did it reject me? How can I feel such warmth and such isolation at the same time? (Underneath this, I'm sure, lurk the same questions I've had, at times, about my own family . . .)

My radiant confusion was deepened and perhaps soured by a naive attitude: to think I switched spiritualties at 16, and left all the rest behind. To think that belief is like citizenship that admits me to one country but bars me from others. To think that a guru can give me a new name and erase the shit and love of my past. To think that because that priest doesn't understand the relationships between the body and ecology, between intimacy and integrity, he is my enemy. After all, he seems to know how to run a soup kitchen with more comfort and manners than I seem to possess.

I didn't really convert. Conversion is a shell-game that obscures your real continuity. The catholic incense of my past will always waft through my yoga studio: how could it be otherwise? It's time to organize things according to usefulness, instead of identity. Useful: re-embodiment, pleasure, community, service, jocularity, inter-generational mentoring, breath, learning, networking. Not so useful: rent economy, priestly hierarchy, dogma, vowed celibacy, funny hats, neurotically repetitive *asana* sequences, disenchanted ritual that no one really feels.

I vow to take the useful wherever it comes. Maybe I'll knit tiny shrouds after *asana* class. I don't have to complicate what needs to be done with questions of who I am. I'm sure I'll never know, and I'm sure it doesn't really matter.

the death of jenna morrison

Jenna was at the heart of Toronto's yoga community and a dear friend of mine. (O Jenna, where are you?) On November 7th of 2011 she was dragged under the wheels of a truck while riding her bike to pick up her son Lucas, who is five. She was five months pregnant. I did a lot of organizing around the tragedy.

I have never seen yoga community come together more closely, and with such speed. Studios set up altars. Soup arrived at the family's door. Yogis got involved in biking and transportation politics. Six weeks after we cremated her we threw a dance party with yoga-aerialists drinking champagne out of a chandelier. We looked up at their sweeping and dangling scarves and we wept for joy.

Studios held classes to raise money for Lucas. Now there are lots of *asana* classes to raise money. At times they may feel like nice gestures only. But sometimes *asana* is the most real and heartfelt thing we can do. Our New Age echoes Patanjali and *Vedanta* with such stinkers as "you are not your body." But when someone dies in this way, we realize this to be nonsense. We are most definitely our bodies, and moving and loving and dancing and touching others is exactly how we experience being alive. Jenna's *embodied relationship* is what has been amputated from those of us left behind. Nobody misses her *purusha*: we miss her signature bum-pinches. It is in bodily absence that we feel our own bodily presence most acutely. Absence makes things real. This life is real, this book is real, Jenna is real, her little man Lucas is real, and we are really here, sharing this. We are all on the edge of not-being. We have no choice but to move and dance and serve, as the *Gita* might say.

I think community arises not only out of the compassion of nonviolent politics and ethical business acumen, but also from the shared paroxysms of grief and joy that shake us without mercy. MWYC needs more death to enter in, that our life may radiate more brightly. MWYC needs more death to stare down our consumer identities, and our loneliness.

During those weeks, I would say to my classes: *Extend your body into any absence you feel — Jenna's, or any other. Align your bones within this emotional chaos. Love this body and those bodies surrounding you, and the time we all exist in, and let's think about how we can love and serve each other better.*

Jenna loved the soup I made: yams, cashews, curry, onion, garlic, and ghee. When I think of her now, I think of stirring the pot with her, in a shared kitchen.

8

Yoga For War:
The Politics of the Divine

Be Scofield

The Tao is called the Great Mother;
empty yet inexhaustible,
it gives birth to infinite worlds.

It is always present within you.
You can use it for whatever you want.

— Tao Te Ching

In the documentary *Yoga Woman,* the world-renowned yoga teacher Donna Farhi stated, "Yoga is one of the most politically subversive practices that any person, male or female, could do in our time." With an estimated 15 million yoga practitioners in the U.S., her provocative statement, if true, could mean significant shifts for a world facing complex global challenges. Beyond this, it raises an important and timely question: What role, if any, can spiritual practice play in social or political change? With ever-increasing opportunities to take the practice "off the mat and into the world," as one yoga activist group phrases it, this relationship between internal and external transformation demands exploration.

For many contemporary yoga practitioners, there's a clear connection between cultivating inner states of peace on the mat and creating a more harmonious and just world. In addition to documented health benefits such as stress reduction, increased fitness, and emotional well being, it's widely believed that spiritual practices such as yoga or meditation can provide grounding for more ethical and wise action. Compassion, kindness, and generosity are just a few of the qualities that many aspire to cultivate on the mat or cushion. In our fast-paced industrial society, these methods offer opportunities to slow down and reconnect, while creating more space for discernment and contemplation of our actions. Through practicing yoga, one can hopefully gain a better realization of the interconnectedness of all things. Many believe, or at least hope, that this renewed sense of awareness will inspire us to take action against injustice in the world.

Undoubtedly, activists can benefit from incorporating some form of spiritual practice into their lives. If nothing else, spiritual practices can help prevent the burnout associated with activism and social justice work. However, what may seem to be an obvious relationship between inner and outer transformation is actually a very complex subject.

The mental and physical benefits of yoga asana are widespread, and would most likely translate across diverse groups. When it comes to the question of how yoga influences ethical and moral action, however, things get complicated. Why? Because any insight gained as a result of spiritual practice must be translated through the unique social, cultural, and ideological frameworks of the practitioner.

An expansive feeling of joy, love, or emotional freedom doesn't equate with any particular political position. Right-wing Republicans and left-wing Democrats can benefit equally from yoga or meditation. Feeling more happy or carefree may inspire random acts of kindness, but it won't change someone's beliefs to reflect any particular political perspective. While a liberal yoga practitioner may say that their practice inspired them to volunteer for a feminist organization, a conservative one may be moved to work for a pro-life group. If the urge to serve people arises from some newly gained insight on the mat, it will be shaped by the context of the individual's preconceived notions. If there's some radical shift in deeply held beliefs, it's just as likely that an ardent pro-lifer would become pro-choice as the opposite.

Spiritual practice alone is therefore inadequate to inform people about the pressing social challenges of the day. Nonviolent Communication founder Marshal Rosenberg warns that privatized, mind/body centered methods such as yoga or meditation may lead people to "be so calm and accepting and loving that they tolerate the dangerous structures." While some spiritual practices may be viewed as subversive or radical because they provide an alternative to the fast-paced nature of the dominant culture, it's important to understand that they can also be consciously or unconsciously used to support the status quo. Engaging in meditation or yoga is no guarantee of distancing oneself from the values, morals, or institutions that shape the surrounding society.

Buddhism and War

In *Mindful Politics (2006)*, Tibetan Buddhist and professor Reginald Ray argues that meditation will make someone challenge the status quo:

> We must understand that meditation, the centerpiece of the Buddhist path, is itself the **most radical kind of political action**. Why? In meditation, we step out of the value system of the conventional world and start to look at things from a fresh viewpoint. We don't know what we are going to come up with, but **we do know we are not likely to remain an uncritical supporter of the status**

quo. Meditation tends to bring out our own intelligence and insight; it encourages our individuality, our sense of outrage, and our
sense of compassion. Meditation is not activism as we usually think
of it, yet it fulfills the definition in a radical way, because it is activity that fundamentally aims to change the world *(emphasis added)*.

Ray reflects a popular understanding of the relationship between spiritual
practice and social change. Many, such as Donna Farhi, assume that a
method like yoga is politically subversive. They believe that through
such spiritual practices, we can remove ourselves from the constraints
of the conventional world. Connecting to what many refer to as the
true self, divine essence, or supreme consciousness is believed to infuse
practitioners with an intelligence or wisdom that's inherently political
and *against* the status quo.

There are, however, some important historical and contemporary examples that challenge this popular conception.

Author and Zen priest Brian Victoria has written extensively on the
role that Buddhism played in supporting the Japanese Imperial Empire
before and during World War II. In *Zen at War* and *Zen War Stories,* he
chronicles the little-known and disturbing history of renowned university professors, Zen masters, and lay monks of many different sects who
gladly assisted their nation in waging multiple "wars of compassion."
The Japanese Emperor was compared to the Buddha, and Buddhist
teachings became an excellent tool to eradicate individualism and dissolve the "small-self" into the larger nation-state. Hitler was jealous:
"Why didn't we have the religion of the Japanese, who regard sacrifice
for the Fatherland as the highest good?"

One of the many people Victoria profiles is Zen master Yasutani
Haku'un. Yasutani was the teacher of prominent American Buddhist
Phillip Kapleau, author of the now classic *Three Pillars of Zen.* While
he received high praise from the likes of Huston Smith and delivered
talks in the U.S., there is another side of him that went untold until
relatively recently.

Although Yasutani's influence on American Buddhism is widely re-vered, Victoria refers to him as a "militarist, not to mention ethnic chauvinist, sexist, and anti-Semite." On the question of Buddhism and killing, Yasutani was unequivocal:

> Those who understand the spirit of the Mahayana precepts should be able to answer this question immediately. That is to say, of course one should kill, killing as many as possible. One should, fighting hard, kill everyone in the enemy army. The reason for this is that in order to carry [Buddhist] compassion and filial obe-dience through to perfection it is necessary to assist good and punish evil . . . This is the special characteristic of the Mahayana precepts.

At the time, Japan was engaged in a cruel war of imperial expansion. This received full support from Yasutani, who stated: "In making China cede the island of Taiwan, and, further, in annexing the Korean peninsula, our Great Japanese Imperial Empire engaged in the practice of a great bodhisattva, a practice that reveals itself through compassion and filial obedience." Yasutani also warned of the demonic ways of the Jews, dismantled liberal reforms, and reiterated sexist statements. He insisted that "the universities we presently have must be smashed one and all," and referred to trades unions and alternative political parties as "traitors to the nation."

Sadly, Yasutani was not a marginal voice. Rather, he was emblematic of how institutional Buddhism wholeheartedly embraced the worst as-pects of Japanese imperialism.

Sawaki Kodo, "one of Japan's best known modern Soto Zen masters and scholars," was a similarly staunch supporter of the unity of Zen and war. "My comrades and I gorged ourselves on killing people," he testi-fied. "Especially at the battle of Baolisi temple, I chased our enemies into a hole where I was able to pick them off very efficiently. Because of this, my company commander requested that I be given a letter of commendation." Another Zen Master, Yamada Reirin, explained how Buddhism shaped his love for the state:

> Wherever the imperial military advances there is only charity and love. They could never act in the barbarous and cruel way in which the Chinese soldiers act. This can truly be considered to be a great accomplishment of the long period which Buddhism took in nurturing {the Japanese military}. In other words, brutality itself no longer exists in the officers and men of the imperial military who have been schooled in the spirit of Buddhism.

Buddhist monks and leaders taught Zazen (sitting meditation) to "discover, through a thorough-going examination of the self, the origin of the power which enabled them, in their various work capacities, to serve the emperor." This, they believed, would allow them to "realize infinite power." When the tide turned against the Japanese, Zen priests abandoned this "thought war" and took positions in factories producing military goods.

Books were also written to defend the Japanese empire. In *The Buddhist View of War* (1937), Komazawa University Professor Hayashiya Tomojiro argued that the Japanese aggression should be seen as "wars of compassion." Stating his strong support for the war effort, Tomojiro insisted that Japanese Buddhists would "as part of our self-sacrificial public duty . . . work for the spiritual general mobilization of the people." The aim of the war, he claimed, was to "save sentient beings and guide them properly."

While these examples are disturbing in their own right, this pairing of Buddhism and war isn't confined to the Japanese Empire. The edited volume *Buddhist Warfare* (2010), clearly illustrates how Buddhism has been used to justify violence throughout its history. In a review of the book, Vladimir Tikhonov notes that:

> From its inception, Buddhism was integrated into a complicated web of power relations; it always attempted to accommodate itself with the pre-existent power hierarchies while preserving a degree

of internal autonomy; and it inevitably came to acknowledge, willingly or otherwise, that the powers-that-be use violence to achieve their objectives, which often overlap with those of the Buddhist monastic community.

Yoga in the U.S. Military

The appropriation of yoga by the American military similarly challenges notions that internal spiritual practices will inspire practitioners to challenge the status quo. In 2006, *Fit Yoga Magazine's* front cover featured a picture of two naval aviators practicing yoga – specifically, *Virabadrasana II,* or "Warrior" pose – on a battleship. At the time, even the editor of magazine admitted that she found this juxtaposition of yoga and militarism a "little shocking." On second glance, however, she realized that "on their faces, their serene smiles relayed a sense of inner calm."

According to Retired Admiral Tom Steffens, the Navy Seals use yoga too. "The ability to stay focused on something, whether on breathing or on the yoga practice, and not be drawn off course, that has a lot of connection to the military," he explains. "In our SEAL basic training, there are many things that are yoga-like in nature." In 2011, the Army added yoga and "resting" to the required physical training regiment in an effort to "better prepare soldiers for the rigors of combat."

With more than 250,000 military personnel struggling with Post Traumatic Stress Disorder (PTSD), yoga is also being used to help veterans recover from the realities of the battlefield. In 2006, the Department of Defense conducted a preliminary study at Walter Reed Memorial Hospital on the capacity of *Yoga Nidra* to heal PTSD. The study found that many of the participants reported less depression and better ability to sleep after several weeks of practice. Yoga teacher Richard Miller, who consulted with the hospital on the study, said the participants "felt more comfortable with situations that they couldn't control, and as a result, they felt more control over their lives." Other studies by the military have shown that "yoga can significantly reduce self-reported symptoms of post-traumatic stress, including rage, insomnia and anxiety." Yoga has since become incorporated weekly at Walter Reed and numerous other military hospitals.

While many practitioners strongly support the incorporation of yoga into the military for humanitarian reasons (such as helping veterans cope with the horrors of PTSD), it's important to recognize that the military's central interest in yoga may be quite different. As the case of the Japanese Buddhists in WWII demonstrates, there's nothing to prevent yoga from being used for purely militaristic purposes. As Admiral Steffens notes, yoga can help soldiers develop their powers of concentration – abilities that, it should be emphasized, are vital to efficiently waging war. Given that an estimated 110,000 Iraqi civilians were killed by American troops over the past nine years, it's important to recognize that training soldiers to utilize yogic powers of concentration does not necessarily represent a humanitarian move.

Corporate Yoga

Yoga has also found a home in another surprising place: the highest echelons of corporate America. As a 2009 Bloomberg article, "Princeton Grad Quits Morgan Stanley to Teach Yoga to Bankers," reported:

> At Morgan Stanley's fixed-income group, Lauren Imparato wore power suits and sold currencies to hedge funds in Europe, Asia and Latin America. Now she spends her days in form-fitting Lululemon pants, teaching yoga to former Wall Street colleagues . . . Imparato's two weekly classes have attracted traders and analysts from Merrill Lynch & Co., Barclays Capital Inc., Morgan Stanley and Goldman Sachs.

Other teachers, such as Sara Harris – who's taught at AT&T, IBM, and NYNEX, among others – specialize in teaching yoga in corporate environments. Harris even adopts her yogic language to include words like "systems" and "mind screens" to better relate to her corporate clients. Today, many major corporations, including Forbes, Apple, Nike, and HBO, offer yoga classes to their employees.

While corporations are not necessarily bad, we need to remember that many of these firms recently defrauded people of millions. As Matt Tabai explains in his article, "Why Isn't Wall Street in Jail?," Wall Street giants including "AIG, Goldman Sachs, Lehman Brothers, JP Morgan Chase, Bank of America and Morgan Stanley . . . were directly involved in elaborate fraud and theft":

> Lehman Brothers hid billions in loans from its investors. Bank of America lied about billions in bonuses. Goldman Sachs failed to tell clients how it put together the born-to-lose toxic mortgage deals it was selling. What's more, many of these companies had corporate chieftains whose actions cost investors billions — from AIG derivatives chief Joe Cassano, who assured investors they would not lose even "one dollar" just months before his unit imploded, to the $263 million in compensation that former Lehman chief Dick "The Gorilla" Fuld conveniently failed to disclose.

Such lawless behavior on Wall Street led directly to the 2008 financial crisis. This, in turn, sparked the ongoing recession that's still hurting millions today.

Many yoga practitioners are staunch supporters of corporate yoga programs on the grounds that corporate employees deserve to experience yoga's health and stress-reducing benefits just like anyone else. (In addition, many teachers simply need such well-paying gigs for personal financial reasons. But that's a different issue.) And this is certainly true. More ambitiously, however, many imagine that teaching yoga to corporate titans might reform problematic corporate practices. Yoga, they predict, will naturally instill a sense of social and ethical responsibility in all those who practice it. Therefore, it's reasoned, nothing could be better for American society than teaching yoga to a rapacious Wall Street banker or cynical K Street lobbyist. But is this really true?

The wildly successful yoga clothing retailer, Lululemon, demonstrates the naivety of assuming that practicing yoga predicts any particular set of social, political, or ethical allegiances. Lulu raised eyebrows among left-leaning practitioners in 2011 when it decided to dramatically emblazon the quote, "Who is John Galt?" on the sides of their shopping bags. Given that the company is renowned for its aggressive marketing methods, which have successfully garnered hundreds of millions of dollars in annual revenue, however, many found quoting right-wing heroine Ayn Rand's *Atlas Shrugged* in such a high-profile way quite fitting. Lulu's founder, Chip Wilson, certainly did: he started the company, he explained, driven by a Randian-inspired "quest to elevate the world from mediocrity to greatness."

Particularly given the increasing trend toward commodification in the multi-billion dollar "yoga industry," this kind of story makes Lululemon the target of fervent criticism. Of course, it's also true that they have a dedicated following as well. People swear by their products despite the hefty price tags. And they either don't care about the company's choice of right-wing political heroines, or actively admire it. Again, this merely illustrates the point that people who practice yoga can and do have vastly different social and political ideologies. A spiritual practice doesn't make anyone more or less likely to embrace American-style capitalism.

The Limitations of Spiritual Practice

If yoga is politically subversive as Donna Farhi claims, why didn't it influence the naval aviators to change their militaristic behaviors? Would the U.S. government incorporate something into the military that could potentially undermine its own objectives? As was the case with Japanese Buddhists during WWII, it seems that spiritual practices may be being used to further violence, war, and political objectives. The presence, mental clarity, embodiment, and focus gained from these practices simply make people *more* efficient killing machines. Similarly, why doesn't yoga help Goldman Sachs' CEO's challenge the status quo? As Gaylon Ferguson states in writing about racism and Buddhism:

> It seems quite clear that, whatever the brilliance of the teachings of the *Buddhadharma*, individual practitioners can continue for years, perhaps lifetimes, with these prejudices left largely untouched by meditation practice. One may even learn to use Dharmic concepts like 'Karma' to reinforce separatism and indifference to the suffering around us.

This profound truth raises serious questions about how spirituality is commonly understood in the North American yoga community today.

Think about all of the white, middle- and upper-class people who have been practicing yoga, meditating, doing visualizations, and chanting in the West for decades now. Has it made them more aware of injustice? More concerned about white privilege or informed about racism? Better educated about poverty? More aware of animal cruelty in the food system? Have the millions of spiritual practitioners subverted anything political? No. Imagine a KKK group who incorporated yoga and meditation. Would it subvert their racism? Change their political consciousness? Would any spiritual practice? No. Rather, because of their cultural context it would merely reinforce their own social and political views. It would make them mentally and physically stronger.

We're all part of larger systems, many of which are incredibly damaging to people and the planet. Along with air force bomber pilots, racists, pro-life extremists, corporate crooks, Japanese soldiers in WWII and (you fill in the blank), we can all experience what we sincerely believe to be spiritual transformation, yet remain oblivious to the dangers of our surrounding culture. In fact, "spirituality" is rather easily incorporated into any social system, including market capitalism, government, and militarism, as a regime of thought control. Richard King, author of *Orientalism and Religion* and co-author of *Selling Spirituality: The Silent Takeover of Religion* captures this sentiment well. "The use of an idea such as 'spirituality' is always bound up with political questions, even when the term is defined in apparently apolitical terms (in which case it supports the status quo)," he notes. "In employing the word, it is important to identify which ideological concerns are being supported."

Spiritual seekers, including yoga practitioners and convert Buddhists, understand the divine, or true essence of reality in a variety of ways. Many believe that God, the supreme consciousness, or emptiness, is supportive, benevolent, or on the side of justice. Of course, it's understandable for someone to think that the universe supports his or her particular beliefs and values. The problem, however, is that many with quite different beliefs and values think exactly the same thing.

As we've seen, countless people have been deeply entrenched in larger systems of violence and domination despite believing they were experiencing connection with the divine through meditation, yoga, or some other spiritual practice. Of course, others have used their spiritual practices and beliefs to resist these same power structures. Therefore, if we assume that there is in fact a divine foundation of reality, it's extremely difficult to see how it wouldn't be morally and politically neutral. If there were a distinct political or moral direction to the divine, and practices such as yoga or meditation were means of tapping into it, then all practitioners would eventually share the same political ideology. This, however, is obviously not the case.

Perhaps it's best to view the potential political subversion of spiritual practices like yoga and meditation as akin to those of psychotherapy. Much healing and transformation can be gained with therapy, just as emotional blockages and wounds can be uncovered and processed on the yoga mat. Experiencing more inner freedom and a vibrant emotional life while being less distracted by habitual patterns or old wounds are outcomes of both. However, it's important to remember that merely growing developmentally or awakening to deeper states of being won't change one's social or political ideology. Yoga and meditation, like psychotherapy, may be effective healing and personal growth practices, but they're politically and ethically neutral.

An Ethical Context

At this point, critical readers might challenge this presentation of "spirituality" as not being authentic, or within the context of a dedicated ethical path. Of course, physical yoga poses, or asanas, are just one aspect of the eight-limbed yogic system. This larger system of yoga also includes the *Niyamas* and *Yamas,* which provide ethical guidelines for personal and social conduct. Similarly, Buddhism has the precepts, which contain specific instructions to abstain from harming living beings, taking things not freely given, and engaging in sexual misconduct, among others. The first response to this challenge is to point out the obvious: the Japanese Buddhists were immersed within this system of ethics, and still wholeheartedly supported war, imperialism, and violence.

Secondly, if ethics are the source for how we determine just behavior, then it's the ethical system – *not* the spiritual practice – that helps decide these issues. Many yoga practitioners, however, tend to assume that quieting the mind and connecting with the "true self" is sufficient to guide ethical behavior. True, a minority of traditionalists continues to insist on the indispensability of the *Yamas* and *Niyamas.* This position, however, would not be found in your average yoga class. Further, there are many, if not more practitioners today who alternatively insist that the feelings generated by the "authentic" self represent the *only* credible guides to ethical behavior we have. While cultivating such inner discernment is, of course, an important means of working through the many ethically complex situations life presents us, the problem with this position is that it tends to throw the baby out with the bathwater. The importance of developing carefully considered personal, and particularly social ethics is dismissed out of hand, supported by the assumption that our innate "inner voice" provides all we need.

Finally, people use ethical systems to meet their own agendas, which reflect their preconceived notions of what is just. The Dalai Lama, who is widely thought of as one of the greatest ethical teachers of our time, has said while homosexuality constitutes "misconduct," having "sexual relations with a prostitute paid by you and not by a third person does not, on the other hand, constitute improper behavior." His ethical system is obviously shaped by his cultural and social context. Another prominent example is Carl Jung, who was intensely interested in issues of mysticism, dreams, psychological growth, and the spiritual. He said, "The Aryan unconscious has a higher potential than the Jewish; that is the advantage and disadvantage of a youthfulness not yet fully estranged from barbarism." His cultural and ethical values clearly shaped his perspectives.

Presence and Justice

Why, one wonders is dissatisfaction with social injustice and a willingness to resist exploitation not seen as a sign of 'spiritual intelligence'?

– Richard King

As we've seen, cultivating presence through a spiritual practice is not by itself an adequate way to address the complex global challenges we face. The "raising of consciousness," as it's popularly phrased in today's yoga and meditation communities, doesn't raise *political* consciousness. An increase in *presence* in the world does not increase *justice*. Nonetheless, these two elements are all-too-often conflated with each other. But inner transformation doesn't necessarily lead to social transformation, despite the popular conceptions to the contrary.

In fact, as Marshal Rosenberg warns, a mere focus on spiritual practice can actually be problematic:

> Unless we as social change agents come from a certain spirituality, we're likely to create more harm than good...The spirituality that we need to develop for social change is one that mobilizes us for social change. It doesn't just enable us to sit there and enjoy the world no matter what. It creates a quality of action that mobilizes us into action. Unless our spiritual development has this kind of quality, I don't think we can create the kind of social change I would like to see.

The activist, writer, and spiritual teacher Starhawk similarly recognizes the limitations of a privatized spirituality. She states, "Transforming the inner landscape is only a first step. Unless we change the structures of the culture, we will mirror them again and again: we will be caught in a constant battle to avoid being molded again and again into an image of domination."

Of course, this doesn't imply that just because a spiritual practitioner gets involved in activism, their efforts will be effective. The compassion, generosity, and kindness that may be learned on the mat don't automatically translate into a well-informed program for social change. Similarly, a dedicated yoga or meditation practice won't make someone a better chef. Certainly, it might increase their presence and focus while cooking. But if the person is a poor cook to begin with, they will remain a poor cook no matter how much yoga and meditation they do (unless, of course, they begin culinary studies as well). The same is true with activism. The mere fact that someone does yoga or is "spiritual" doesn't mean that he or she will be a knowledgeable activist. Being a good activist requires understanding power dynamics, forming relationships, and being aware of the ways in which privilege can reproduce some of the problematic structures and dynamics one aspires to change.

Two great examples of successful activists that combined spiritual practice with work for justice are Martin Luther King, Jr., and Thich

Nhat Hanh. They met in 1966 after Hanh had written an open letter to King explaining the reasons for several self-immolations by Buddhist monks in Vietnam. King subsequently nominated Hanh for the Nobel Peace Prize. He stated in his letter to the committee that: "His ideas for peace, if applied, would build a monument to ecumenism, to world brotherhood, to humanity." They are both lasting inspirations for those seeking to engage in spiritual activism.

Dr. King was very cognizant of the structures and institutions that were perpetuating injustice in his time (the most damaging of which, it should be noted, are still very much with us today). His life and career were dedicated to transforming them. King moved himself and his family into the slums of Chicago to protest *de facto* segregation in the North, organized a massive march on Washington to achieve guaranteed income and jobs, and was assassinated while working alongside striking sanitation workers in Memphis, Tennessee. He spoke out against capitalism, racism, and war, and was a fervent critic of U.S. foreign policy.

King did all of this as a religious leader. He claimed to have meditated an hour a day and enjoyed spending frequent time in nature. As a Baptist minister, he also spent much time in prayer. He wrote sermons about the importance of introspection and reflection before designating people as enemies and formed strong and lasting relationships with those he was working with during the struggle. Furthermore, King actually spoke of the importance of action, and not relying solely upon God or faith to do the work.

Hanh, who has dedicated his life to socially engaged Buddhism, worked tirelessly during the Vietnam War to bring an end to the conflict. The organization he founded, the School for Youth and Social Services, rebuilt villages, established health care facilities, and built schools. Hanh led this organization in a non-partisan manner, and refused to take sides in the war. Thus, he provided his services to both the North and the South Vietnamese. Furthermore, he campaigned in the U.S. to support the anti-war movement and to convince the government to withdraw. Today, Hanh continues to teach the importance of both embodying peace through spiritual practices *and* working for change in the world. He reminds us of our interconnectedness and inspires us to see the larger web of existence in which we live. This spirit is captured in Hanh's interpretation of the second precept of generosity:

> Aware of the suffering caused by exploitation, social injustice, stealing, and oppression, I vow to cultivate loving kindness and learn ways to work for the well-being of people, animals, plants and minerals. I vow to practice generosity by sharing my time, energy and material resources with those who are in real need.

There are no simple answers to the complex global challenges we are facing on this earth. However, it is helpful to understand the extent to which spiritual practices like yoga can — and cannot — guide our efforts at social transformation. This conversation around the relationship between internal and external transformation will undoubtedly continue as more and more people feel the urge to bring a world out of balance back to equilibrium.

9

Our True Nature is Our Imagination: Yoga and Non-Violence at the Edge of the World

Michael Stone

Being firmly grounded in non-violence creates an atmosphere in which others can let go of their hostility.

—*Yoga Sutras* of Patanjali, Chapter 2, Verse 35

I'm trying to stay warm as I type on my silver laptop at the corner of Cedar Street and Liberty Avenue, the park at the heart of the Occupy Wall Street movement. It's freezing in the shade and I'm facing a sign that reads: "Economics for Activists Meeting at 3 p.m." I've returned from an hour in the People's Kitchen helping three volunteers get a portable camping stove working under a wet brown tarp. A truck is unloading a massive heap of sleeping bags and blankets that have been donated by a local church, and behind a row of police someone is cleaning the altar whose centerpiece is a photograph of John Lennon. Meditation was at 7 a.m., cleaning at 8. Yoga was cancelled because it's raining. It's October 28th and a *New York Times* reporter is reminding the group of people who are going to speak that today is the day that the world's population hits seven billion. If you're twelve years old, the world's population has grown by one billion in your lifetime.

A rising population set to grow without end puts enormous pressures on a planet that's already falling into environmental catastrophe. Providing food, clothing, shelter, and energy for seven billion people is a task of startling complexity. While the economists and ecologists are searching for ways to solve the climate crisis, I'm trying to imagine what the yoga tradition can offer us at this time. Because if the great tradition of yoga has anything to offer our culture – now is the time.

I'm here at Zuccotti Park, but not with the cliché arsenal of a yoga mat or meditation cushion. Instead, I'm trying to learn how the activist community, the spiritual community, and the economists can build bridges. Instead of attending the public yoga class, I've been learning about General Assemblies, the human microphone, hand signals, and what kind of research is needed to generate sweeping changes that bring attention and help to the unwanted parts of our society, as well as to our overall ecology. It feels like I'm trying to build a bridge at the end of the world. The bridge begins right here at the People's Kitchen as we try and string tarps over the stove, the small media centre, and the People's Library, where 300 books were donated yesterday.

Dreaming of a New Model

This isn't the first time that I've come out to protest. But it is the first time that I've really felt that as a person committed to the yogic values of interdependence, non-violence, and community, I can't support a growth-based capitalist economy that's destroying the biosphere and taking us all with it. For our economy to maintain equilibrium, it has to grow by at least three percent per year. This means our economy will double in size within 24 years. Our oceans, atmosphere, and the stress on sentient life can't take this.

I know capitalism doesn't work well on a whole range of dimensions. And I know we can do better. But in the world of social change I've also seen many supposed left models fail as well. And as far as I can tell, none of the models have done well at answering the questions of how to expand democratic self-rule and self-governance. Do we know how to govern ourselves as citizens who care about the health and longevity of our planet, and the beings that inhabit it? Can we acknowledge and deal with the divisions within the so-called "99 percent" that have historically divided our movements, understanding the way that racism, patriarchy, nationalism, and hetereonormativity intersect with self-organization and self-rule?

A man stands on a bench and chants a phrase from a meeting last night: "We don't want a higher standard of living, we want a *better* standard of living." He's wearing a crisp navy blue suit and typing tweets into his iPhone. Next to him, Slovenian philosopher Slavoj Žižek, wearing a sweaty red t-shirt, is surrounded by at least 100 people as he makes his way onto a makeshift platform.

Since the protesters aren't allowed to use megaphones or amplifiers, they have to listen carefully to the speaker's every sentence. After each one, the speaker pauses, and those close enough to have heard repeat it in unison for those farther away. It's called the human microphone. When Naomi Klein spoke three nights ago, some sentences were repeated four or five times as they echoed through Liberty Park and down Wall Street, passed along like something to be celebrated and shared, something newborn.

Slavoj Žižek chants:

They tell you we are dreamers. The true dreamers are those who think things can go on indefinitely the way they are. We are not dreamers. We are awakening from a dream which is turning into a nightmare. We are not destroying anything. We are only witnessing how the system is destroying itself. We all know the classic scenes from cartoons. The cat reaches a precipice. But it goes on walking. Ignoring the fact that there is nothing beneath. Only when it looks down and notices it, it falls down. This is what we are doing here. We are telling the guys there on Wall Street — Hey, look down!

A Movement, Not a Protest

We are awakening from a dream. Modern yoga is also a collective awakening and it will be interesting to see if we can transition from a personal practice into a collective voice for social change. We all suffer from the increasing paradox of living in a time whose old ways and values are dying (and taking waterways, species, languages, and air quality with it) while the new one seems unable to be born. Stopping in our tracks, like we do in meditation practice, begins the slow unraveling of our momentum so we can see what is here to emerge.

I realize that I'm participating in a movement, not a protest. This is a movement because we are dreaming big. Instead of listing popular demands like "tax the rich," we're trying to call on our imagination to articulate another narrative for how we can live together.

It's here that yoga may have much to offer. This is also a spiritual movement. At the core of this revolution lie the same values that anchor the yoga tradition: non-violence, compassion, interdependence, awakening, suffering, and deep listening.

Over and over, Patanjali teaches that what causes suffering is holding on to inflexible views. The stories that govern our lives are also the narratives that keep us locked into set patterns, habits, and addictions. The same psychological tools that yogis have mapped for helping us let go of one-track rigid stories can be applied not just personally, but socially.

When we begin to open to the nature of our lives, the spectrum that's revealed includes both peace and pain. Humans are always trying to gain pleasure. A commitment to the various meditative paths of yoga is a commitment to opening to the way that our lives really are. As we open to feelings that move through the body, old wounds arise. And as we move closer to those wounds, we have to work with the distractions that keep us from really dropping into what we feel.

Under our deepest habits and compulsions, we don't enter some empty void or blissed out paradise – we enter the world. And the world right now is in distress.

Yoga teaches us that as we open to our lives, we open to suffering and pain – not just our own, but the suffering of all beings. *Yes,* we heal internally; *yes,* we find more ease in our lives; *yes,* we are less stressed. But the paradox of practice is that although we feel more free internally, we also become more sensitive to the pain of others. And from there, we begin to take action.

If we don't take action, the yoga process is incomplete. If our teachers fall to the side of passivity, they are complicit in maintaining the status quo – where, in our era, we aren't serving the truth of climate change and economic injustice. "If you think spirituality and politics are separate," Gandhi once quipped in an interview, "you understand neither spirituality, nor politics." Enlightenment, I would add, is the ultimate cognitive dissonance. On the one hand, we find freedom in our own lives. On the other, we're more attuned to the interconnectedness of life. And if others are suffering – so are we. So, at some point in practice, we turn around and begin serving others. (And altruism aside, serving others is more fun!)

This is the great tragic paradox of being alive. Our lives are so precious, and the sunrise on Hudson River is breathtaking; the world is a catastrophe, and meeting families who've had homes foreclosed is painful. If we lose track of the pain of others, we also lose track of our lives.

No matter how modern yoga has become, consciousness is still rooted in intimacy. No matter how much we believe we can be free through individual practice, that freedom is always tethered to the freedom of others.

Broken Systems

Protests emerge from the social fabric when traditional forms of debate and participation are blocked. Just like symptoms emerge from the body when the meridians are dammed, the same forces work in society. The sense of injustice, in short, is not just about the unfairness of a small part of society living in unimaginable wealth, while so much of the rest lives in economic desperation. The issue in the U.S. is not just about the top 2,000 American households with more income than the poorest 24 million. It's about the degradation of politics that turns wealth into power through campaign financing, lobbying, and the revolving door between business and government. Vast inequality and the accompanying sense of injustice explain why the protests have also exploded in Chile and Israel, two countries that are doing relatively well in terms of economic growth and employment.

Our social, health care, and economic systems aren't working as they should. The upper one percent of Americans are now taking in nearly a quarter of the nation's income annually. Their wealth has increased astronomically. Yet we have way too many people without jobs. It's not just the vast wealth at the top that Occupy Wall Street protestors are questioning, but how it was earned and is being used. As I travel through the United States and parts of Europe (especially Greece), I'm shocked at the number of people who are unemployed at a time when there are so many needs to fulfill. And there are too many homeless. Homelessness and unemployment is terrible for the digestive system and immune function of our families, children, and communities.

This is not to say financial markets aren't important. They are not inherently bad. Our financial markets are supposed to allocate capital and manage risk. However, what they actually did was misallocate capital and create risk. Now we're bearing the cost of their misdeeds.

We can't socialize losses and privatize gain. "They took risks," the Nobel Prize winning economist Joseph Stieglitz tells me at Zuccotti Park, "but nobody took the money away from them." Standing in line for soup at the People's Kitchen, a collective cooking for those of us camping at the corner of Cedar Street and Trinity Place, Steiglitz describes the economics of hoarding: "Asymmetric Incentives," he calls it.

A man behind me overhearing our conversation says, "The banks preyed on the poorest Americans. This is predatory investing."

Mindfulness, Intimacy, and Meaning

In Patanjali's central definition of yoga, yoga is defined as "the cessation (*Nirodha*) of [the misidentification with] the modifications (*Vritti*) of the mind (*Citta*)." What kind of "cessation," we must ask, is Patanjali actually referring to here? He's certainly not suggesting that the mind comes to an end. The nuance of this classical statement has to do with clinging.

When we don't stick to the feelings, images, and thoughts that move through awareness, we are practicing yoga, which I translate as intimacy or embeddedness. Not clinging to fixed and rigid views is the heart of intimacy. If you and I sit together, and as you speak, my mind is distracted with associations, ideas, turbulent emotions, or small fantasies about how your boots remind me of someone I used to know and the way we once had an apartment together and how she kissed and that one time when I caught her . . .

When I'm caught up in my attachment to ideas and stories, I'm not connected with you. Patanjali calls this *Smrti*. *Smrti* is a verb that means "to remember." In English, we call it "mindfulness." It means to be mindful of what's happening now, to recall what's important, and to come back to this moment – to your life. So as I practice not clinging to what moves through awareness, a space is opened that was previously obstructed by my busy mind. Paradoxically, non-attachment is engagement.

Ecological understanding focuses on the limitations associated with closed systems, such as our planet. The inherent physical limitations of such systems define sets of parameters within which the system can maintain relative homeostasis. If it moves too far beyond them, the system will break down. So, for example, from the ecological perspective, carbon dioxide levels in our atmosphere must not be allowed to rise too high – or else global warming will reach a tipping point beyond which the Earth's ecosystem will rapidly deteriorate and no longer be able to support complex life.

A closed-system perspective, such as the ecological paradigm, reminds us that our actions make a difference. This is called karma. Everything we do has an effect. Furthermore, our actions are meaningful because they make a difference.

Shifting Stories

The media love a good fight. In Toronto during the G20, those not involved in the protests were eventually distracted by images of a burning police car in the banking sectors. With burning cars and young men breaking windows, there was suddenly a more entertaining target than the real issues of policies determined to impose new austerity measures, but ignore impending climate catastrophe. With violent images prevailing, the protests lost momentum because the issues were forgotten in the media.

This time, even though there is a massive police presence at most protests, the movement is not giving the media the images of broken windows they love. Instead, we're seeing a blossoming of creativity and hope.

We need a language now that allows us to reimagine what a flourishing society looks like. Any meditator knows that there are times when the thoughts that stream endlessly through awareness can eventually grow quiet. But it's only temporary. The stories come back.

But they return differently. They have more space and they are more fluid, less rigid. We need stories to think and make sense of a world — an ailing world that needs us.

A convenient way to apply the Buddha's message to the social sphere is to remember that viewpoints never end or dissolve altogether. Rather, we learn to shift from one story to another, like a prism being turned, so that the possible ways of looking at our lives can constantly change. It's time to adapt to our economic and ecological circumstances — uncomfortable truths we've been avoiding for far too long. This awakening is not just about economics. It's equally about ecology and our love for what we know is valuable: community, healthcare, simple food, and time.

This process of dislodging old narratives is the function of both spirituality and art. Both ethics and aesthetics ask us to let go in a way that is deep enough that we find ourselves embedded in the world in a new way. If we think of this emerging movement as a practice, we'll see that as it deepens, and we let go of habitual stories, our embeddedness in the world deepens as well. Intimacy deepens. Relationships deepen.

In the same way that moving into stillness is a threat to the part of us that wants to keep running along in egoistic fantasies and distraction, those with the most to lose are going to try and repress this outpouring of change. They'll do this with police, of course. But they'll also use more psychologically manipulative measures, like calling us communists or anti-American, anti-progress, etc. Our job will be to keep a discerning eye and watch for rhetoric that attempts to obscure what we are fighting for.

These protests are reminding us that with a little imagination, a lot can change. We are witnessing a collective awakening to the fact that our corporations and governments are the products of human action. They aren't serving us anymore, and so it is in our power and in our interest to replace them. We aren't fighting the people on Wall Street; we're fighting this whole system.

Collectively Imagining the Future

We have a painful journey ahead of us. We don't yet know how it will emerge. Nobody can guess the future. But with some courage, we can imagine one.

First, sustainability requires a change of technologies – in farming, energy, industry, transport, and building – so that each of us is putting less environmental stress on the planet. Global co-operation will be crucial is transitioning from coal, oil, and gas, to an era powered by low-carbon energies such as sun and wind. Sustainable technology begins and is supported by a change of values.

Second, we need to stabilize the global population and voluntarily reduce fertility in the poorest countries. This will involve keeping girls in school, excellent education, and healthcare.

Third, we need a way to slow down and return to values of relationality and interdependence. This is where yoga comes in. Yoga teaches us that we are much happier when we serve others. Self-centered happiness is an oxymoron.

I have no idea how we can do this as a community yet. But I'm learning. Day by day, we can foster generosity and altruism in our families and with our friends by letting go of actions and old stories that focus on "me first."

Being able to change our mind *is* enlightenment. Maybe being able to change the structures within and around us is the activation of our deepest, hard-won insights. Wisdom and action can't be separated. To imagine yoga as an internal and private experience is only half the picture. If we are to serve the fish and waters and homeless in our communities, we need to take our action to the streets and watersheds. In this way, the streets and watersheds become our altars. We offer to them our imagination, our time and devotion. Devotion is the expression of intimacy and self-centeredness is its enemy.

Žižek, the protestors, and Patanjali share a common and easily forgotten truth: we cause suffering for ourselves and others when we lose our sense of connectedness. We are the 99 percent, but we are dependent on the one percent that controls 40 percent of the wealth. Those statistics reflect grave imbalance in our society. So of course people are taking to the streets.

This movement is also showing the power of non-violence. Non-violence, a core precept in my own yoga practice, is not an ideology. It's the power of facing what's actually going on in each and every moment, and responding as skillfully as possible. The depth of our awakening, our humanness, has everything to with how we care for others. Our sphere of awareness begins to include everything and everyone. The way we respond to our circumstances shows our commitment to non-harm.

Emerging from the Gaps

But what causes this shift? How did Cassie, a 20-year-old woman with no experience as an activist, organize 2000 people to come help clean up Zuccotti Park when Mayor Bloomberg tried to evict us? What motivated Saheera, an African American woman from the Bronx, to help organize Occupy the Hood, a conversation among the black populations in the New York suburbs that hadn't heard of the protest, or imagined it as exclusive to white middle-class men unhappy about unemployment? What motivates us to drop what's comfortable and act for the commons?

In meditation practice, we can experience gaps between the exhale and the inhale, between one thought dissolving and another appearing.

The space between thoughts is the gentle and creative place of non-harm. The meditator learns to trust that quiet liminal space with patience. Because from it, new and surprising ways of seeing our lives emerge. This is the inherent impulse of non-harm in our lives. It begins when we bear witness to the fading of one thought and emergence of another.

These protests are exposing the gap between democracy and capitalism. The way democracy and capitalism have been bound is coming to an end. We want democracy, but we can't afford the runaway growth economy that isn't benefiting the 99 percent. And if the 99 percent aren't benefiting, the truth is that the one percent are affected too. If there's anything that we're all aware of these days, it's that it's not just Twitter and e-mail that connects us – it's water, speculative banking, debt, and air as well. When the one percent live at the expense of the 99 percent, a rebalancing is certain to occur.

If we can trust in the space where, on the one hand, we are fed up with economic instability and ecological degradation and, on the other, we value interconnectedness, we are doing the same thing collectively that the meditator does on his or her cushion. We're trusting that something loving and creative will emerge from this space that we create. As I write this in November 2011, it's too early to say what that may be. It won't just be a rehashing of an ideology from the past. These are new times and require a new imaginative response.

When the wealth of a society becomes asymmetrical, the wealthy are less likely to allocate money for basic needs like healthcare, housing, food, and infrastructure. We're seeing how this works in healthcare and education – there's less need for the one percent to spend on, or even support, national healthcare or excellent public education, when they can purchase it privately themselves. As this way of relating to society becomes entrenched, the one percent and 99 percent lose track of each other. Compassion declines. From a Buddhist perspective, this harms us all. The laws of interdependence hold that we need each other and live more meaningful lives when we care for each other.

Restraint, Imagination, and Generosity

The people of Occupy Wall Street – and now Occupy San Francisco, Toronto, Montreal, Boston, Copenhagen and 1,900 other cities – are trying both to take over public space that's being wrested from the people and hold the possibility of a new way of living. What's been stolen is not merely physical space (foreclosed homes, for example) but space to rethink how our society operates – and what to do about the bottom dropping out.

Even the media, looking for a hook, can't find one. "What are your demands?" they keep asking. The answer: "It's too early to say." Let's see how much space we can hold; let's see what our power is. Then we can begin talking about demands.

If we're going to fully express our humanity and wake up as a collective, we need to replace our youthful ideas of transcendence with the hard work of committing to the end of a way of life in which our actions aren't in line with our values. According to the foundational platform of yoga, homelessness and poverty are bad because they involve *Dukkha*. We are trying to end *Dukkha*. So spirituality and economics must come together.

It's important for spiritual communities to understand that society's emphasis on the accelerated accumulation of capital undermines yoga's most important teachings. In yoga there are five ethical precepts. This morning at Occupy Wall Street, I wrote them out for Jeffrey Sachs, a leading economist curious about how yoga could contribute to a new economics:

Ahimsa: Recognizing that I am not separate from all that is. This is the precept of non-violence.

Satya: Listening, acting and speaking from the heart in each spontaneous circumstance. This is the precept of honesty.

Asteya: Being satisfied with what I have. This is the precept of not taking what is not freely given.

Brahmacharya: Encountering all creatures with respect and dignity. This is the precept of the wise use of sexual energy.

Aparigraha: Using all the ingredients of my life without clinging. This is the precept of non-greed.

Restraint and imagination underpin all the precepts. To live without being greedy is not just to live without being greedy for things. It's about being generous: generous with your time and your face and your imagination. Sometimes I want to replace this last precept and simply say: take refuge in the imagination. To literally re-imagine the way you see the world, over and over again, as an act of generosity to your own mind, and the minds of others; to your own heart, and the hearts of others. I think ethics are a great way into the imagination. You need a strong imagination to hold your emotions. You need a strong imagination to hold what you think of as your life.

These days, I find that most of us don't talk about healthy imagination. We do talk about health. Are you healthy? How do you get more healthy? That's what most people want. Health. I think it would be interesting the next time you think about your own health to also think about the health of your imagination. What can you do to create elasticity there? Because if there's some way for us to work in the fissures of our economy and ecology right now, it's going to be with our imagination. We have to re-imagine a Western life style that's more sustainable.

Fearlessness is a way of not being greedy, to not be scared of giving someone your face. Giving your face is like having a steady hand. You just give someone your face. Giving your face is also like giving an honest answer, an honest response. You can do this with everyone, even people who are locked up, who you've locked up, or who are dying.

If you've ever been with someone who is dead, it's really nice to give your hand to a dead person. I remember when my uncle died nobody was there. I didn't know what to do and that was my hand's response.

Just being able to sit with him, holding the hand of someone who was dead still felt like giving. This is the inter-being level, the imaginative level, of *Aparigraha*: not being greedy, not being stingy, not being possessive. Having generosity. Giving. Giving fearlessly.

No Division Between What and How

Here in Zuccotti Park. I have no idea what to do when I arrive and I have no idea where this is going. Like everyone else, I have doubts. So I talk with people. I help cook. I give my attention, my face. This is how movements begin: eating together, giving our bodies attention, recognizing the needs of others, pioneering new modes of communication, and reimagining a world in the heart of the one we don't believe in anymore.

This movement is not about making demands. What is yogic about this movement is that it's trying to articulate an entirely different narrative about how we can live. It's *showing* the possibilities in the diverse ways that it's organizing. This is the social dimension of yoga — a dimension we need in order to re-imagine our lives. We've been underselling America and what's possible. For me, the beauty of Occupy Wall Street is that it's pushed me into a new space where I've been asked to be patient and trusting, where I focus more on process and less on immediate outcomes.

I didn't know what to expect coming here. What I thought was impossible is becoming inevitable. We are capable of so much. It's amazing to see the hunger for radical ideas and deep connection. The squares are joyful and there's no sense of coercion. People want to be here, bring friends, and come every day. It's amazing to see people getting a taste of a new way of living.

Our main problem isn't being under the threat of predatory investing. It's that we haven't trusted in our imaginations deeply enough to have confidence in what's possible. I don't know where any of this is going. I hope this moment turns into a sustained popular movement that eventually builds systems to speak for itself. It's inspiring to dream big. And given the global response, it seems appropriate.

In a yoga framework, the division between what you're doing and how you're doing it isn't acceptable. In this framework, it matters how, what, why, and where you're doing what you're doing. All those levels matter. The reworking of the idea of karma from this perspective is that it's not just what your intention is in how you do your work that matters. Your actions actually make a difference. It does matter what you do. Your actions have to make a positive difference.

It's easy to say that your intentions are really pure. You find a little bird on the ground. You pick up the bird, kiss it, and feed it organic seeds. (I'm sure there's an app for when you find a bird.) You take the bird home, put it on a raw diet, and cuddle it. And then you find out that the bird got kicked out of its nest so it could learn how to fly. You've just interrupted the whole process with your good intention. You didn't get it; you didn't see the cycle. Your intentions were good, but your actions were not so skillful in the grand scheme of things. This is the dance of *Aparigraha*. This is what puts you into your life.

We're demanding a fundamental change of our system. Yes, we all need to work through our individual capacity for greed, anger, and confusion. This is an endless human task. We also have to stop cooperating with the system that breeds greed and confusion as it shapes our lives and our choices. This movement is the beginning of bringing that system to a halt. From here, anything is possible.

10

How Yoga Messed With My Mind

Angela Jamison

Santa Monica in 2001 felt like the crux of Kali Yuga. The dark age of the spirit. That's where I got into yoga.

Daily practice cured me of headaches and back pain and eased a noxious variety of postmodernism. These results came the first year; for six more, I kept practicing. A sociologist by trade, I filtered Los Angeles yoga culture through a "scientific" approach to practice. But that systematic, dispassionate practice, it seems, eventually undermined my hardheaded rationalism. I honestly know less now than I once did about why yoga is so effective for so many people, myself included. But I do have some fun stories to tell so far.

Los Angeles

I moved to Los Angeles in 2001 to train in seeing the familiar in the strange, and the strange in the familiar. That's how C. Wright Mills described soft science, in the methodological treatise where he urges young sociologists to keep notebooks on every social world they encounter. Having deconstructed hard science as an undergraduate proto-philosopher, I went to UCLA to learn some gentler research methods — statistics, archival research, and ethnography — and to get a Ph.D. The following paragraphs build from my old Mills-inspired yoga notebooks, since the person who wrote them is gone now — replaced by someone she might have found decidedly . . . strange.

For most people, immersion in the turn-of-the-century Los Angeles yoga world would offer far more strangeness than familiarity. I like to imagine what Bodhidharma would see there. Or Krishnamacharya. Or my grandmother. My particular conditioning included 18 years off the cultural grid on a rural Montana ranch, a family of devout Christians shut away by conservatism but also blown open by service, four years of liberal arts amid earnest and brilliant Portland hipsters, two years obsessed with revolution and liberation theology in Central America, and one year as an independent media activist and non-profit administrator in Seattle.

So while not naïve, I was still stunned by what was going on in yoga studios all over the West Side from 2001 to 2008. Someone told me that we could change the world by "doing this," when "this" was stretching in a group while listening to Sheryl Crow. The spiritual books people applied to their lives were *The Secret* and *The Power of Now*. I saw a man deeply impress a woman by claiming that the parking space opening in front of us on Venice Boulevard was the result of his "manifestation" powers. Twice, upon learning that I studied luxury consumerism, yoga people told me that their SUV's "didn't count" because they were hybrids. At the *Whole Foods* checkout in Brentwood, I'd see friends on the cover of the *Yoga Journal*; later, at the studio, there would be grousing about who got selected to model this month.

At the time, I was learning to think more like Pierre Bourdieu, the sociologist who sees social life as a series of overlapping fields of activity in which we more or less unconsciously compete for position. So to a degree I observed the yoga world dispassionately, taking the strange/familiar experiences simply as information – as data. My own participant-observation made me as good a data point as any other.

But for the training in semi-objectivity, there were things that got past my ethnographer lenses, and shot straight to the gut. Language strongly shaped the shared and the subjective experiences we were having, and given my worldview, the lexicon I respected was minimalist, precise, and unemotional.

So I remember the way my throat and belly would contract whenever an otherwise sincere practitioner or teacher detached from (what I considered) her *real* embodied experience and reverted to language of "energy," "chakras," and "auras." It appeared that these tawdry old New Age concepts were used to self-mystify and mythify, making one's own experience more vague.

This seemed dishonest (which was a bit of a moral issue), but – more obviously – metaphysical language seemed self-serious, quasi-religious, and unfunny. I longed for the ironic self-awareness so plentiful in nearby lifeworlds.

Besides what I took as leftover hippie dialect, most of the late 20th century's airy New Age yoga had retreated to the nearby hills (specifically, Topanga Canyon) by 2001. The new vibe was distinctly postmodern: centerless, anti-authoritarian, and morally relativist.

At YogaWorks, everyone in a room of 40 was asked to define yoga. The only answer cited more than once was "when I feel really good." Three senior teachers told us we were all correct. In other words, yoga was whatever a person wanted it to be: for *her*. It was personal. One had a right to say what yoga was for her; she did not have a right to say what it was for someone else.

While I was starting to detect a peculiar, western interpretation of *Advaita Vedanta* in the Ashtanga yoga subculture, in the big Los Angeles yoga scene I only saw so-called "nondualism" regularly in two sorts of discourse. First was the frequent claim that body and mind are literally one entity, so that "working on the body is also working on the mind." The second was the claim that all negative thought and emotion was a projection of one's own mind. The idea worked like this: *if I think another person is fearful, this is only my own fear coloring my perception. I know nothing of other minds, because in fact they do not exist. My consciousness generates my reality all by itself.*

Meanwhile, in my academic practice, the big ideas were dying. More talk about theory (which I loved) didn't help me understand daily human life. Since now I had 12 hours a day to study, I started to spot the contradictions in these theories, and to write in a way that stood on its own ground rather than references to bigger thinkers. To my dismay, 21st century social science wasn't about big ideas at all.

This is why I didn't take a reflexive interest in my own bias against certain yoga language. That bias harmonized with science's do-what-you-can empiricism, and with its finger-in-the-dike rationalism. But I did critique the postmodern and "nondual" tendencies I saw all over West Side yoga in those days, even while I ironically played with those notions to test their usefulness and open my own mind. Perhaps those critiques are still useful, so I'll over-generalize them below.

Most obviously, the moral relativism of "yoga is anything you want it to be" was not only potentially irrational – treating yoga as a wish-fulfillment machine likely to contradict itself – it was also oddly moralistic. Strong definitions of yoga were actually not allowed. Moreover, I started to notice that the fear and hatred of authority that colored interpretations of past generations – particularly anything related to 19th century yoga gurus – was related to a broader distrust of hierarchies and authority. So while the message that yoga was anything you want it to be was freeing, it also blocked out traditional, non-customizable definitions of yoga. And this message sometimes had reactive, fearful undercurrents.

When it came to so-called nondualism (the claim that all social and physical reality takes place in the field of one's own mind), this sometimes led to a series of rather vain conclusions, especially given the availability of Botox and plastic surgery. The idea that others' minds were one's own "projections," instead of articulating Hindu insights into the nature of human psychology, was more often used to refuse to really listen to one's boyfriend. It was also a good excuse for breaking up with guys who didn't do yoga.

How I Practiced

My mind was crazy: sharp, hyperactive, infused with self-defensiveness and over-confidence. And my way of defining and doing yoga was heavily conditioned by arbitrary situations, habits, and beliefs. So it is extremely strange that a practice of moving and breathing (or often just sitting) was able to hold my attention steady for long enough that deep beliefs and ways of perceiving began to break down. Here is how that happened over the first seven or eight years, or about 12,000 hours.

Despite my scholarly practice of taking the Los Angeles yoga world as just another social field, another part of me saw it as very, very special. The fact was that something *beyond* sociology was also going on there — something I couldn't figure out alone or find in just any cultural milieu. The fact was that this world transfixed me. For all its troubles, it was laced with a kind of human experience more interesting than any I'd contacted before.

I tried hard not to be mystified. But asana practice brought out a raw honesty, equanimity, and consistency that I'd never been able to figure out in other venues. From the start of my daily practice, my intimates and I liked the clear-minded Angela. But she was an alien.

I had been a person who cruised on cleverness and chased every last intellectual delight. I was ravenous for knowledge, experience, and change. Like many academics, I used quick-fly analytical skills to cover for an attention span shorter than most dogs'. But when I quit my academic job in 2010, my husband said that from the start my yoga practice had an odd "integrity" about it — a quality he hadn't seen anywhere else since we met at age 18.

Here is how I came to practice daily. In 2002, I was crossing a street, and a woman talking on the phone drove into me. My right hand and hip smashed into her hood; and then it was my chin that made first contact with the pavement. After that, I just remember blackness. When I woke up, a needle was going into my arm. I wiggled and told the EMT I didn't put drugs in my body; she told me I was paralyzed from the neck down. My body-mind did as suggested. I spent the night at the University's ICU, much of it lashed to a board, unable to move or feel my body below the neck. My husband eventually got my hands to feel his. The next morning, I walked out with a headache and an overwhelming case of gratitude. In coming days, having a body got *really* interesting.

I had been taking asana classes regularly for a year, enjoying every class I could find, but as I moved into daily practice, I wanted a silent form. This is because, as long as I did not have to put my attention on a teacher, and if there was little auditory distraction, my discursive mind would shut off during asana practice. The experience was wonderful, but at the time I had no idea how to let it happen outside of an Ashtanga yoga room.

Now that I teach yoga, I am even more mystified that asana practice enabled me (someone with low kinesthetic intelligence and no understanding of meditation) to shut off the discursive mind from day one. Most people do not experience such a split between practice mind and everyday mind. In any case, what's not surprising is that this experience of asana practice quickly led to sitting practices, and to the 8-limbed model of yoga practice.

But at the moment I was ready for daily Ashtanga practice, the Los Angeles yoga scene was spinning into crisis. The founders of YogaWorks sold their school to a large fitness corporation and began planning a move to Hawaii. Their hundreds of devoted students began scattering to start new enterprises, or taking up different forms of practice. This churn continued through the first years of daily practice, as all the experienced teachers on the West Side underwent mini-uprootings. There was no consistent, experienced teacher on the West Side for more than a few months at a time.

Teacher-Method-Community

What happens to the tender baby practitioners when a Western yoga community goes to pieces? I would submit that, whenever this happens, some will likely take the trauma as a blessing. If they do, they'll grow stronger than they would have otherwise, and more sensitive to the importance and beauty of whatever yoga community they can possibly find.

It was horribly sad to see my new teachers and friends mourn the loss of their community and teachers. Yet I was not hurt in the same way others were, because I had not learned to depend on the same resources. I resolved to learn something – anything – from the disintegration. I looked to the few remaining old-timers for guidance, and took their words so to heart that I still hear them in my head. One mentor told me that a practitioner needed three supports – community, method, and teacher. Another said that it was understood that a person had to practice a decade before beginning to teach. I concluded that, without a consistent teacher or strong community, the method itself would have to be my main support. Even as – years later – I gained a global community, and met a senior teacher, this commitment to clear method remained.

This three-fold structure that shows up in many religious forms – a harmony of checks and balances that supports any kind of practice in its preservation, celebration, and continuation. Call it what you will – the "triple gem," the "three-legged stool," first/second/third person perspectives. For me, and now for many of my students, it has been a useful model thus far.

Other Supports for Practice

Maybe because I was short on community and teacher in the early years, I seem to have built some of my practice theology out of the belief systems closest to hand: science and Christianity.

Science gave me the humbling and inspiring idea that yoga was a modern experiment. Each practitioner produced data for an inquiry that was far bigger than just her. To contribute to the cumulative knowledge of yoga, I reasoned, I needed to meet Patanjali's minimum specification that practice happens (*Sutra* 1.14) "for a long time, in earnest, without a break." I continue to draw energy from the notion that my practice is a data vector in the grand design of *Dirga Kala*: the last day I skipped an asana practice was April 2003. In that it still works, I take the idea to be true.

Drawing on Christianity was harder, because I had to keep what I was doing hidden from myself. For many years, I continued to believe that I'd lost my religion at 18, when I stopped eating meat and started reading David Hume. I read all about the sociology of religion, but at first could not see how modern yoga was – while not a formal religion – a religious form. When my mother cautioned me never to quiet my mind during yoga because this would allow demons to come in, I laughed over it with my friends, noting how funny it was that a scientist like me would come from the world of folkways and superstitions. (Six years after that conversation, I would meet my first demon up close near an Indian burial ground, and realize the ways my mother had been right.)

But my parents and grandparents all inhabited Christianity with rhythms, emotions and consistency that supported me from a distance. For example, my father (a hospital chaplain) used to insist that we read one Psalm and one Proverb before breakfast every single morning. (Much of that repressed scripture flooded back into consciousness on my first silent retreat in 2004). A gratitude junkie, he shouts "thanks Lord!" several times a day when he notices something beautiful in the world. And he lives the notion that faith without works is dead.

I did not see how deeply my emotional body is patterned to imitate my father until halfway through a three-month practice retreat in India in 2010. Over the course of two weeks, I came to see my habitual feel-ing-tone toward practice as a transitive, impersonal state-of-being that could show up anywhere, at any time. I could summon this receptive, gratitude-fueled, diaphragm-trembling thrill at most any time *if* yoga practice was involved, be that anything from a 4:15 a.m. asana session to a motionless two-hour sit. But this peculiar pattern wasn't *mine* — it was an embodied state that could just as easily be infused into some other self. In fact, it was from another person that I had first learned it before I could walk or talk. It was my father's emotional signature for many of his conversations with God.

Losing My Religion Again

By now it has become impossible to write this story as if yoga is only a science, and as if I still believe vague language is bad style, if not bad character. It is difficult to say anything about the last four years of my practice without using the word *energy*, if not the dreaded *chakra, aura,* and *spirit*.

It's not unusual for even the most "scientific" long-term meditator to trip into what my meditation teacher Shinzen Young calls the "spirit realms." When a person spends a *lot* of time in *Pranayama, Pratyhara,* or meditation, old thought patterns simply crop up and begin to wind themselves down. This is as predictable as the way old injuries resurface and heal through asana practice.

Beyond that, one might come across stranger experiences of the kind the lesser-read *Yoga Sutras* describe. Patanjali and most spiritual teachers will urge that paranormal experiences are not special, and are nothing to go chasing. My own practice has been to avoid them as much as possible, because my teachers see them as sources of potential delusion, and because they undermine my hard-won sense that I sort of know what yoga is.

There are layers of consciousness — many of them — that I could not even fathom for the first many years of daily practice. I've come to realize that it is worth working with people who understand consciousness deeply — teachers more experienced and clear-minded than my "inner guru." It might be worth considering that yoga is not just anything we want it to be, so that it can fulfill our most obvious needs.

Between these fairly predictable astral or spirit dimensions, and the more mundane mental patterns that come up in meditation practice, my awareness has settled on a field that can only be called *energetic*. Because of repeated, usually unwanted, encounters with the weirder spirit realms, I've come to feel relatively normal about building out my awareness in the field of experience that the yoga tradition calls *Pranamaya Kosha*. "Energy" no longer seems a metaphysical word or a purely subjective category. It simply refers to a whole world of shared, even visible kinetic process. Perhaps, all those apparently spaced-out hippies I was talking to in Santa Monica a decade ago already inhabited the energetic dimension I am only now beginning to perceive. They were just generous enough to talk with me about chakras and auras years before I had felt or seen them.

I have a feeling that yoga can learn from contemporary meditation communities in which more esoteric experiences are discussed openly, free of the secrecy, mystification, or repression that characterized most traditional forms of practice. While speaking openly about esoterica does create a potential distraction for new practitioners, it also might keep yoga humble enough to grow quickly and strongly beyond our current "dark age." It might get us all thinking that yoga is not just whatever we want it to be.

Afterword

The Evolution of Yoga and the Practice of Writing

Roseanne Harvey

The most fitting way to conclude this book is to reflect on how it came to be.

21ˢᵗ Century Yoga began on a warm September evening in 2011, when I received an email from Carol Horton with the subject line, *idea for a collaborative project.* It was an invitation to co-edit "a book called something like *North American Yoga: Critical Perspectives on Contemporary Practice*":

> The theme would be along the lines of: most writing about con-
> temporary yoga is either technical (instructing you how to do asana)
> or philosophical (generally focused on traditional Indian thought).
> Lately, there have been some new additions to the field - books on
> yoga history, and yoga memoirs.

What we are lacking are books that take an in-depth look at yoga as it currently exists in North American society. It's wildly popular and hugely profitable - and it's paradoxically used for everything from weight loss to spiritual transcendence. What is this weird postmodern phenomenon?

This group of writer/practitioners weighs in, focusing on how yoga relates to a diversity of issues including politics, business, spirituality, Buddhism, psychology, post-colonialism, consumerism, and social activism.

My response was simply, "yes yes yes!"

These are all things I love, so of course I would want to be part of such a project. I explore the intersection of yoga, politics, activism, and contemporary culture often on my blog, *It's All Yoga, Baby.*

I strongly believe that writing about yoga is an essential practice right now. Modern yoga is at a very interesting place and needs to pause for reflection. Yoga is at a precarious juncture where it could go in a number of directions. As practitioners and as a community, we have the opportunity to co-create the future of yoga. Reflection, writing, and dialogue are necessary components of this process.

One of my favorite books about yoga is *How We Live Our Yoga,* a collection of personal stories edited by Valerie Jeremijenko in 2001. In her introduction, she wrote, "Where are we as a nation in our romance with yoga? Is our heady infatuation over? Are we reaching a place where we can settle down to quietly discuss it?"

Kind of. I'm not sure if we've settled down to "quietly discuss" yoga. If anything, the dialogue is more boisterous than ever. Teachers and practitioners have started talking, and there has been an explosion of books, feature magazine articles, and blogs about yoga. Blogging especially has contributed to the growing conversation by introducing many sophisticated, educated, and passionate voices to the mix.

The immediacy and reach of blogging is wonderful. But we also need to slow the conversation down so that we can contemplate where we are right now. Carol and I have been part of an online community that's exploring many fascinating ideas about yoga, many of which resonate with our own thinking. *21st Century Yoga* embodies our desire to draw out these ideas, expand them, and preserve them in book form.

Yet writing about yoga is almost a paradox. What kind of words can describe the intimate, visceral, esoteric experience of yoga? Yoga emerged from a pre-literate culture. The teachings were passed on through storytelling. Patanjali's *Sutras* are so concise and crystallized because they were memorized, recited, and passed along orally. Eventually, the scriptures were written down. But for centuries, they were an oral tradition.

Similarly, the North American "canon of yoga literature" doesn't have a long history. Until about 15 years ago, among the few available books on yoga were Iyengar's *Light on Yoga,* Yogananda's *Autobiography of a Yogi,* and Richard Hittleman's *Yoga: 28-Day Exercise Plan* (which you can still find in second-hand book stores around the continent). Most of the books on the market were instructional manuals and translations of scriptures. There were even fewer books about practice and modern culture.

In the mid-twentieth century, Carl Jung, Luce Irigaray, and Aleister Crowley, among others, wrote about yoga. But their writing was often buried in collections and not accessible to the average practitioner. It could easily be argued that writing about modern yoga didn't really take off until 1976, when *Yoga Journal* was conceived by a group of California yoga teachers that included Judith Hanson Lasater. With *Yoga Journal* and succeeding yoga publications came the creation of a market for writing about yoga.

The "canon of yoga literature" has continued to grow in recent years, with a proliferation of yoga memoirs, cultural histories, and how-to books. Still missing, however, was a collection of voices that delved into the complexities and paradoxes of contemporary yoga practice and politics. *21st Century Yoga* is an attempt to fill that empty space and take the conversation — so currently vibrant in the yoga blogosphere — to the next level.

Integration of Process and Product

Although I now identify as a blogger, my background is in magazine and book publishing. I love the process involved in print: reading, editing, discussing, revising, developing ideas, organizing words and sentences, and finally, sending it all to the printer. Then waiting.

I was editor of the leading Canadian yoga magazine, *Ascent*, which published its final issue in 2009. The magazine introduced me to blogging, as we installed a blog in 2007 only to find – like every other magazine that had done this at the time – that we had no idea what to do with it. I quickly grew to hate the blog. As *Ascent* had a small staff, the task of maintaining the blog landed on me, along with editing the entire magazine.

At first, the blog was an annoying task that added to my already huge workload. It never flowed. We spent a lot of time trying to figure out what to do about it. Then the magazine went out of business and I found myself unemployed. With my abundance of free time, I decided to start my own blog: *It's All Yoga, Baby.* The name is a reference to the main coverline of the final issue of *Ascent.*

I started the blog because it was easier and cheaper than starting another magazine. I thought it would be a way to stay connected to the many teachers, writers, and artists in the North American yoga community that I had encountered through the magazine.

The blog ended up achieving this goal, and serving many other purposes as well: pushing my thinking about yoga, expanding my concepts of what the practice can be, sparking conversation, tapping into a dynamic and interesting community, and making new friends. Through the blog, I've been grateful to discover a lively assortment of interesting people and encounter impassioned discussion about all aspects of yoga practice. My community expanded beyond Montreal across Canada, around North America, and beyond.

I encountered all of the voices in this collection in the blogosphere. I read their writing on their own blogs or "blogzines" such as *Elephant Journal* and *Yoga Modern.* Even Carol and I met each other through our blogging activity.

The intention of *21st Century Yoga* is to bridge the immediacy and relevance of the blogosphere with the deeper thinking and conceptual development possible in a collection of essays. We wanted to push the thinking and writing found in the blogosphere and refine it through the editing process – which has the ability to strengthen and reinforce ideas and arguments.

I love the immediacy and relevancy of the online world. But I also see the value in an old-fashioned book (even if read on an e-reader). Books are timeless and tangible. They're a holding place for ideas and thoughts to percolate, to be easily revisited at a later date. The old-school publishing process allows for the gift of other sets of eyes, feedback, and rigorous dialogue. The book form (paper or electronic) is a testament to the thought and process that go into good, intelligent, reasoned writing.

Since Carol and I both come from the democratic and (mostly) open-source systems of the blogosphere, it was a natural choice to self-publish *21st Century Yoga*. We didn't even try approaching publishers or agents. We consciously chose to avoid the traditional publishing route, which is based on old, hierarchal systems. We wanted the final product to reflect the collaborative process of creating the book.

21st Century Yoga is even made possible through crowdfunding, an alternative fundraising economy. We raised the money to design the cover and interior of the book through a campaign on a platform called Indiegogo. Within 36 hours of launching the campaign, we reached our $2,000 goal, proving that there is a hunger in the yoga community for writing about yoga that is critical, challenging, political, and relevant to life in the 21st century.

I experienced the process of co-editing this book as fitting somewhere between the scheduled rigor of magazine production and the fearless exploration of a group blog. Our structure allowed for editorial process and the refinement of ideas, supported by a collaborative, subversive, DIY spirit. And with no need to worry about upfront expenses or book sales because of the print-on-demand model, as editors we were able to encourage contributors to take intellectual and personal risks, to open and bare themselves.

The Politics of Practice

Like most everything in my life, my yoga practice has evolved over time.
I began when I was a student at the University of Victoria in British
Columbia, signing up for a yoga class and practicing in a gym with 25
other people, led by an endearing middle-aged woman with long red hair.

I continued to pursue yoga on my own a little bit, and then went
to live in the UK. I bought a Sivananda yoga book and practiced in the
dark little room I rented in a house in Bristol. I didn't realize it at the
time, but I had returned to yoga because I felt uncomfortable, awkward,
and foreign all the time. I was depressed and homesick, and my yoga
practice helped relieve my pain.

I practiced intermittently over the years, taking sessions here and
there through my 20s, fitting it between my travels, crappy work experiences, and messed-up relationships. But I didn't really commit to yoga
until I made the radical decision to move to an ashram in southeastern
B.C. when I was 28, after being hospitalized for the most serious bout
of depression of my life.

I needed a place to heal and think about my life, and the ashram seemed
like the perfect place to do that. I also needed to work. While I was receiving medical benefits and wasn't healthy enough to hold down a regular
job, I had energy and wanted to feel like I was contributing. The ashram
was a working community. Karma yoga, the practice of working without
attachment to results, was what the community practiced together.

It was also a writing community. People carried around notebooks
and could be found writing on chairs, benches, in waiting areas around
the ashram. I already had a life-long writing practice, which ebbed and
flowed with whatever else was going on; so I found this to be my element. (I had also written a lot while I was in the hospital; there were
many striking similarities between the hospital and the ashram, which I
will write about another time).

On my first morning at the ashram, I rolled out of my little bed at 6:35
a.m., slipped on some clothes, and walked through the winter darkness to

the main building for the morning yoga class. I was surprised when after the opening *Oms,* the teacher asked us to take out our notebooks. We did some yoga poses, she asked some questions, we wrote down our answers and we continued this rhythm for the rest of the class. This was my introduction to what's known as "Hidden Language Hatha Yoga."

This was the first time that I had experienced yoga and writing as complementary practices. After spending time at the ashram, I moved to Montreal to edit *Ascent,* and the two practices (along with the ever-important practice of work) continued to interrelate. And with a chronic back injury that's aggravated by many asana postures, writing (and particularly writing about yoga) has become my primary practice.

As I've investigated my own writing practice and immersed myself professionally in yoga culture over the past decade, I've watched the themes and conversations that have emerged in the North American yoga community. Some have been important, inspiring, provocative, and creative. Others have represented questionable, ridiculous, and just plain inaccurate expressions of the practice.

New Ways of Writing and Thinking About Yoga

So what is this weird postmodern phenomenon that we call "yoga"? I don't feel any closer to understanding what yoga is than I did when I started editing this book. As Carol points out in her Introduction, the contributors don't subscribe to a singular definition of yoga. At times, even their attempts at defining it are contradictory.

Julian Walker writes, "We get to define what yoga means for us in the 21ˢᵗ century." Angela Jamison, however, points out the danger in thinking yoga is whatever we want it to be, based on her own experience with the practice. "My way of defining and doing yoga was heavily conditioned by arbitrary situations, habits and beliefs," she notes.

This multi-dimensional conversation about the practice embraces the paradoxes and inconsistencies of yoga, and gives equal weight to some of the different, but equally valuable voices and perspectives therein. The greatest gift of this collection is the willingness of the contributors to ask questions and be open to answers – to wonder, explore, and not-know.

As Matthew Remski observes, yoga "wants self-expression and constant redefinition. Young and dumb and full of possibility, yoga is also looking in the mirror, wondering how it looks." If there's one thing that yoga cultural watchdogs, scholars, and teachers agree on, it's that this millennial-old practice is still in its adolescence in the West.

Just as it's important for my well-being to have the time and space to reflect on my life, it's essential that yoga as a modern practice takes the opportunity to do so as well. In a sense, the blogging community is yoga's journal, where yoga explores itself and reflects. *21st Century Yoga* complements this ongoing online discussion by taking ideas found there, crafting them into much more in-depth essays, and compiling them in book form. It's important for yoga culture to hold space for deepening dialogue and discussion. This helps the evolution of the practice, steering its direction and the future course of contemporary yoga.

After spending months reading drafts of the pieces in this collection, I find myself feeling hopeful about the direction in which yoga is going. What I see in this collection is a fearless exploration of personal experience, an investigation of which can help us collectively navigate the challenges of postmodern life. In particular, I'm optimistic that we are close to reaching a place where we are open to even more respectful discussion and collaboration.

Obviously, I'm biased. But I do believe that *21st Century Yoga* has something unique and groundbreaking to add to the evolving "canon of yoga literature." My wish is that there will be successors and subsequent volumes. There is much to question and explore, still. Closing this edition with no singular definition or conclusion means the conversation is only beginning.

Acknowledgements

Tremendous thanks to Sheryl Lilke-Cooper, who copy-edited the *21st Century Yoga* manuscript and made invaluable editorial suggestions. Heartfelt gratitude to Sarit Rogers, who conceptualized, shot, and produced the arresting photographs gracing our front and back covers. Thanks also to yoga teacher Keri-Anne Telford and her husband, artist Joe O'Neill, who served as the yoga models featured in Sarit's photos. Deep appreciation to Drew Fansler for creating the powerful designs featured on the book cover. And tremendous thanks to our 72 IndieGoGo contributors, whose financial support and well wishes underwrote our production costs and boosted our spirits. Of this group, extra special thanks are due to Andrea Craig; Anne-Lisa de Forest, founder of Namaste Productions, Montreal, Canada; and Ted Grand, co-founder/director of Moksha Yoga, Salt Spring Island, BC, Canada; whose exceptional generosity demonstrated their faith in the value of this project, and provided much appreciated support.

Contributors

Poep Sa Frank Jude Boccio is a certified yoga teacher, interfaith minister, member of Thich Nhat Hanh's Order of Interbeing, and Zen Buddhist Dharma teacher ordained by Korean Zen master, Samu Sunim. His book, *Mindfulness Yoga: The Awakened Union of Breath, Body, and Mind* is the first to apply the Buddha's mindfulness meditation teachings to yogasana practice. Besides his writing appearing in *Tricycle, Shambhala Sun, Namaskar,* and *Yoga Journal,* he maintains two blogs: *Mindfulness Yoga* and *Zen Naturalism.* Based in Tucson, where he lives with his wife, Monica, their daughter Giovanna, and their two cats and two chickens, he travels worldwide, leading workshops and retreats.

Roseanne Harvey is a writer, editor, and yoga teacher in Montreal. As the former editor of *Ascent* magazine, she has been situated at the intersection of yoga and media for more than six years. Her blog, *It's All Yoga, Baby* is known for questioning, provoking thought and shining a critical light on yoga culture ~ while celebrating community, service, creativity, the independent spirit, and good ol' fun. She is co-director of Yoga Festival Montreal and a passionate community organizer.

Carol Horton is a writer, consultant, and yoga teacher. She holds a Ph.D. in Political Science from the University of Chicago and served on the faculty at Macalester College in St. Paul, Minnesota. Since leaving academia to live in Chicago with her husband and start a family, she's worked as a research consultant in the nonprofit sector, specializing in programs affecting low-income families. A Certified Forrest Yoga teacher, Carol teaches yoga to women in the Cook County Jail with Yoga for Recovery. She is the author of *Race and the Making of American Liberalism* (Oxford University Press, 2005); and *Yoga Ph.D.: Integrating the Life of the Mind with the Wisdom of the Body* (Kleio Books, 2012).

Angela Jamison is the founder and owner of Ashtanga Yoga: Ann Arbor, a traditional Ashtanga Vinyasa yoga school. Each year, she takes retreat in India for one to three months. Her Ashtanga teacher is R. Sharath Jois, and Shinzen Young guides her sitting practice. She has been writing about yoga at insideowl.com since 2006. A former sociologist, she holds degrees in philosophy, journalism, and history, and is ABD in Sociology at UCLA. She spent most of her life on a ranch in rural Montana, and now lives in Michigan with her husband Rob Jansen and their cats, Lynxx Moon and Zelda Spoonbender.

Melanie Klein is a writer, speaker, and professor of Sociology and Women's Studies at Santa Monica College. She is the adviser of the Santa Monica College Leadership Alliance, and founder and co-coordinator of Women, Action + Media! Los Angeles. Melanie attributes feminism and yoga as the two primary influences in her work, and is committed to consciousness-raising, promoting media literacy, healing distorted body images, and cultivating healthy body relationships. Founder of the blog *FeministFatale,* her work may also be found at *Adios Barbie, Elephant Journal, Ms. Magazine's* blog, and *WIMN's Voices.*

Matthew Remski is writer in the morning, therapist in the day, and teacher in the evening. His writing includes poetry, novels, posts, and fragments, focusing on yoga, ayurveda, and evolution. As a therapist, he holds space for people as they illuminate the shadows of body and heart, informed by his knowledge and training in ayurveda, yoga, psychotherapy, and philosophy. Matthew teaches courses in ayurveda and yoga philosophy based upon his ongoing research of writing, and experience of practical therapy. He also teaches yoga asana, primarily in a therapeutic context. With Scott Petrie, he is the co-creator of the *Yoga 2.0* project, and co-director of Yoga Community Canada. He blogs at www.matthewremski.com.

Chelsea Roff is a writer by day and yoga teacher by night, a weaver of words as well as of asanas. Currently Managing Editor at *Intent.com,* her writing has appeared in *Yoga Journal, Elephant Journal,* and *Yoga Modern.* Chelsea is passionate about using online media to inspire action that serves a greater cause, and travels the country writing about how modern yoga is evolving in the most non-traditional of spaces — from festivals to public protests to centers for at-risk youth. In Dallas, Chelsea helped start a service organization that brings yoga to people in homeless shelters, juvenile detention centers, and prisons. She currently lives in Santa Monica, California.

Tommy Rosen is a certified Vinyasa Flow and Kundalini yoga teacher, and a leading authority on addiction and recovery. He is a pioneer in the relatively new field of Yoga and Recovery, which utilizes yoga and meditation to help people move beyond addiction and build fulfilling lives. Tommy teaches yoga at Naam Yoga L.A. and Bhakti Yoga Shala, and runs workshops and retreats internationally. He is the co-founder of Tadasana International Festival of Yoga & Music in Santa Monica, California, and teaches and speaks regularly at yoga conferences and festivals including Tadasana, Wanderlust, Hanuman, and Bhaktifest. His writing has been featured in the *L.A. Yoga, Yogi Times, Aquarian Times, Huffington Post, Daily Love,* and *Yoga Mint.* Tommy lives with his wife, noted yoga instructor Kia Miller, in Venice, California.

Be Scofield is a certified yoga instructor, founder of godblessthewholeworld.org, beyondwhiteness.com, and Dr. King scholar. He writes for

Tikkun magazine and *Alternet.org,* and is an anti-racist educator and social activist. Be is studying to be an interfaith minister at the Graduate Theological Union in Berkeley, where he recently taught a graduate course called "Dr. King and Empire: How MLK Jr. Resisted War, Capitalism and Christian Fundamentalism."

Michael Stone is a yoga teacher, Buddhist teacher, author, and psychotherapist. He is the Founder of Centre of Gravity, a community in downtown Toronto integrating everyday formal practice and social action. He is a voice for a new generation of young people synthesizing spiritual practice with environmental and social issues. His most recent book is *Awake in the World: Teachings from Yoga and Buddhism for Living an Engaged Life* (Shambhala 2011). You can find him online at www.centreofgravity.org.

Nathan Thompson has been practicing yoga, primarily Iyengar-based, for more than a decade. He is a long-time member of Clouds in Water Zen Center, where he received the Dharma name Tokugo (Devotion to Enlightenment) in 2008. He is the author of the spiritual and social justice blog, *Dangerous Harvests,* as well as the conscious relationship blog, *21st Century Relationships.* Nathan has also written articles for a variety of online and print publications, and has a regular column at the webzine, *Life as a Human.* He lives in St. Paul, Minnesota.

Julian Walker lives in Los Angeles. He is a writer who has been teaching yoga since 1994, maintains a busy bodywork practice, and leads retreats, workshops, and teacher trainings. Julian is passionate about mythology, poetry, psychology, music, free-form dance and authentic communication. He calls himself an "activist for reality-based spirituality" and explores the integration of science, spirituality and embodied psychology in a forthcoming book, *The Embodied Sacred: Spirituality Beyond Superstition.* More information about Julian's classes, workshops, teacher training, book, articles, and CDs can be found on his website, www.julianwalkeryoga.com.

References

The following contributors to *21ˢᵗ Century Yoga* wish to acknowledge the works listed as important sources of quotations, ideas, and information. Citations follow the sequence in which they appear in each chapter.

Julian Marc Walker, "Enlightenment 2.0: The American Yoga Experiment"

Sri Swami Satchidananda, *The Yoga Sutras of Patanjali: Commentary on the Raja Yoga Sutras* (Buckingham, VA: Integral Yoga Publications, 1990)

Walt Whitman, *The Complete Poems* (NY: Penguin Classics, 2005)

Edmund Wilson, *The Shock of Recognition: The Development of Literature in the United States Recorded by the Men Who Made It* (NY: Modern Library, 1943)

Henry David Thoreau, *Walden* (Los Angeles, CA: Empire Books, 2011)

Henry David Thoreau, *Civil Disobedience* (Los Angeles, CA: Empire Books, 2011)

Henry David Thoreau, *Selected Essays, Lectures and Poems - Ralph Waldo Emerson* (NY: Bantam Classics, 1990)

R. M. Bucke, *Cosmic Consciousness* (NY: Penguin Arkana, 1991)

Lorin Roche, *The Radiance Sutras* (Marina Del Ray, CA: Syzygy Creations, 2008)

Mark Singleton, *Yoga Body: The Origins of Modern Posture Practice* (NY: Oxford University Press, 2010)

Coleman Barks, *The Essential Rumi*, New Expanded Edition (NY: Harper One, 2004)

Robert Bly, *The Soul is Here for Its Own Joy: Sacred Poems from Many Cultures* (NY: Ecco, 1999)

Dan Siegel, *The Neurobiology of "We": How Relationships, The Mind and The Brain Interact to Shape Who We Are* (Louisville, CO: Sounds True, 2008)

Melanie Klien, "How Yoga Makes You Pretty: The Beauty Myth, Yoga and Me"

Susan Bordo, *Unbearable Weight: Feminism, Western Culture and the Body*, 10th Anniversary Edition (Berkeley, CA: University of California Press, 1993)

Virginia L. Blum, *Flesh Wounds: The Culture of Cosmetic Surgery* (Berkeley, CA: University of California Press, 2003)

Stuart Ewen, *Captains of Consciousness: Advertising and the Social Roots of the Consumer Culture* (NY: Basic Books, 2001)

Georg Feuerstein, *The Shambhala Encyclopedia of Yoga* (Boston: Shambhala Publications, 1997)

bell hooks, *Communion: The Female Search for Love* (NY: Harper Collins Publishers, 2002)

Jean Kilbourne, *Can't Buy My Love: How Advertising Changes the Way We Think and Feel* (NY: Touchstone, 1999)

Sharon Lamb and Lyn Mikel Brown, *Packaging Girlhood: Rescuing Our Daughters from Marketers' Schemes* (NY: St. Martin's Press, 2006)

C. Wright Mills, *The Sociological Imagination* (NY: Oxford University Press, 1959)

Peggy Orensetein, *Cinderella Ate My Daughter: Dispatches from the Front Lines of the New Girlie-Girl Culture* (NY: Harper Collins, 2012)

W. James Potter, *Media Literacy* (Thousand Oaks, CA: Sage Publications, 2012)

Erich Schiffman, *Yoga: The Spirit and Practice of Moving Into Stillness* (NY: Pocket Books, 1996)

Jessica Weiner, *Life Doesn't Begin 5 Pounds From Now* (NY: Simon Spotlight Entertainment, 2006)

Ganga White, *Yoga Beyond Belief: Insights to Awaken and Deepen Your Practice* (Berkeley, CA: North Atlantic Books, 2007)

Naomi Wolf, *The Beauty Myth: How Images of Beauty Are Used Against Women* (NY: Harper Collins Publishers, 2002, 1991)

Frank Jude Boccio: "Questioning the "Body Beautiful": Yoga, Commercialism, and Discernment"

William J. Broad, "How Yoga Can Wreck Your Body," *The New York Times Magazine* (Jan. 5, 2012)

"Yoga by Equinox," YouTube (Dec. 27, 2011) *http://www.youtube.com/watch?v=loszrEZvS_k*

Kathryn Budig, "Stop Judging and Read," *Huffington Post* (Jan. 17, 2012)

Shelly Grabe, Monique L. Ward, and Janet Shibley, "The Role of the Media in Body Image Concerns Among Women: A Meta-Analysis of Experimental and Correlational Studies," *Psychological Bulletin* 134, no. 3 (May 2008), 460-476

Jennifer L. Derenne and Eugene V. Beresin, "Body Image, Media, and Eating Disorders," *Academic Psychiatry* 30 (2006), 257-261 *http://ap.psychiatryonline.org/article.aspx?articleid=50181*

Vickie Rutledge Shields, *Measuring Up: How Advertising Affects Self-Image* (Philadelphia: University of Pennsylvania Press, 2002)

Wilhelmina Mauritz Shoger, *The Unattainable "Reality": How Media Affects Body Image in Men and Women and the Moderating Effects of Social Support*, Doctoral dissertation, Illinois Institute of Technology (2008)

Ophira Edut, *Body Outlaws: Rewriting the Rules of Beauty and Body Image: The Book That Redefines Beauty* (NY: Seal Press, 2004)

Nathan Thompson, "Bifurcated Spiritualities: Examining Mind/Body Splits in the North American Yoga and Zen Communities"

J. Brown, "Nonviolence, Hypocrisy, and Veganism" *http://idproject.org/blog/j-brown/2011/9/27*

Sandy Boucher, "Making Our Way: How Women are Embracing the Dharma and Challenging Buddhism's Status Quo," *Buddhadharma* (Winter 2010)

Susan Griffin, "Ecofeminism and Meaning," *Ecofeminism: Women, Culture, and Nature* (Bloomington, IN: Indiana University Press, 1997)

B.K.S. Iyengar, *Light on Life: The Yoga Journey to Wholeness, Inner Peace, and Ultimate Freedom* (Emmaus, PA: Rodale, 2005)

Carol Krucoff, "Insight from Injury," *Yoga Journal* (June 2003)

Reginald Ray, "Touching Enlightenment," *Tricycle* (Spring 2006)

Chris Saudek, "Interview with Geeta Iyengar" (1995) *www.iyengar-yoga.com/articles*

"*Yoga Journal* Releases 2008 'Yoga in America' Market Study," *Yoga Journal http://www.yogajournal.com/advertise/press_releases/10*

Be Scofield, "Yoga for War: The Politics of the Divine"

msnbc.com, "Soldiers learn to loosen up with yoga" (July 16, 2006) *http://www.msnbc.msn.com/id/13890826/ns/health-fitness/t/soldiers-learn-loosen-yoga/*

Anna Mulrine, "Army's New Physical Training Incorporates Yoga, Resting," *Christian Science Monitor* (March 4, 2011) *http://www.csmonitor.com/USA/Military/2011/0304/Army-s-new-physical-training-incorporates-yoga-resting*

Katie Drummond, "Inside the Pentagon's Alt-Medicine Mecca, Where the Generals Meditate," *Wired* (Dec. 23, 2011) *http://www.wired.com/dangerroom/2011/12/pentagon-alt-med-mecca/*

Iraq Body Count *http://www.iraqbodycount.org/*

Nancy Wolfson, *Incorporating Yoga http://www.yogajournal.com/lifestyle/294*

Matt Tabai, "Why Isn't Wall Street in Jail," *Rolling Stone* (Feb. 16, 2011) *http://www.rollingstone.com/politics/news/why-isnt-wall-street-in-jail-20110216*

Richard King, *Selling Spirituality: The Silent Take Over of Religion* (NY: Routledge, 2005)

Gaylon Ferguson, "No Colors, All Colors," in Melvin McLeod, ed., *Mindful Politics: A Buddhist Approach to Making the World a Better Place* (Somerville, MA: Wisdom Publications, 2006)

Carl Jung (William McGuire and R.F.C. Hull, eds.), *C. G. Jung Speaking: Interviews and Encounters* (Princeton, NJ: Princeton University Press, 1987)

Dalai Lama, *Beyond Dogma: Dialogue and Discourses* (Berkeley, CA: North Atlantic Books, 1996)

Marshal Rosenberg, *The Heart of Social Change: How You Can Make a Difference in Your World* (Encinitas, CA: Puddle Dancer Press)

Starhawk, *Dreaming the Dark: Magic, Sex and Politics* (Boston: Beacon Press, 1982)

Thich Nhat Hahn: "The Precepts" *http://www.thebigview.com/buddhism/precepts.html*

Index

Made in the USA
Charleston, SC
24 October 2012